GROW GREAT GRUB

Organic Food from Small Spaces

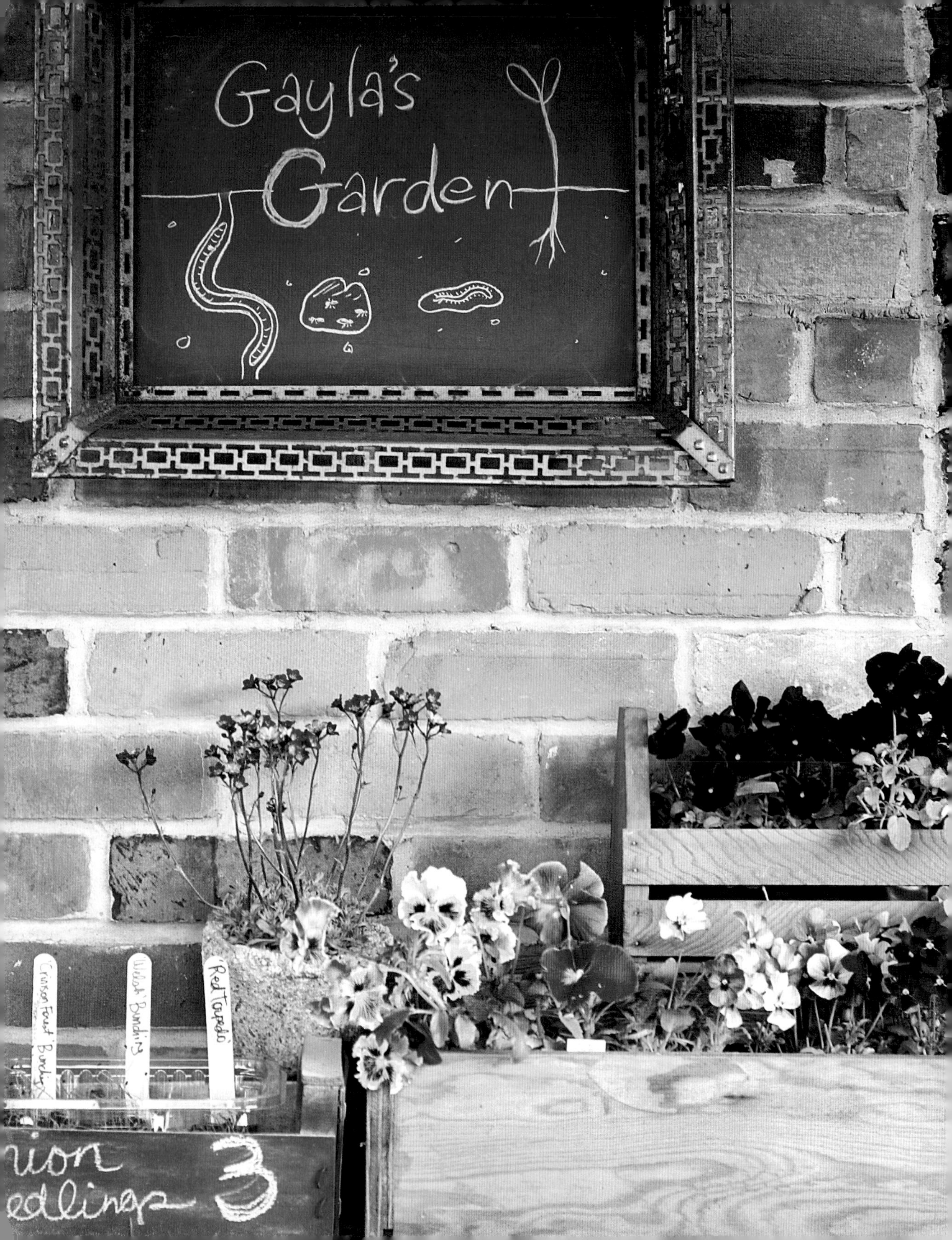
Gayla's
Garden

GROW
GREAT
GRUB

Organic Food from Small Spaces

from the creator of *You Grow Girl*

Gayla Trail

Clarkson Potter/Publishers
New York

Published in the United States by Clarkson Potter/
Publishers, an imprint of the Crown Publishing
Group, a division of Random House, Inc., New York.

www.crownpublishing.com

www.clarksonpotter.com

CLARKSON POTTER is a trademark and POTTER
with colophon is a registered trademark of Random
House, Inc.

Library of Congress Cataloging-in-Publication Data
is available upon request.

ISBN 978-0-307-45201-6

Printed in China

Design by Fluffco

10 9 8 7 6 5 4 3 2

First Edition

To Davin, my partner in
making fresh food and a
homegrown meal.

Contents

Introduction: Becoming a Microfarmer

As a child I was introduced to the possibility of urban agriculture when I saw a bucket of potatoes growing on my West Indian grandmother Scylla's tiny concrete balcony. Making a new life in an apartment in the cold Canadian north did not stop Scylla from continuing to grow her own food as she had at home in Barbados.

The discovery of that bucket led me to experiment with my own less-than-perfect garden spaces so many years later, and inspired me to begin to push the accepted norm of what a garden is and where it can exist.

I built my first "real" vegetable garden in the tiny, garbage-filled backyard of the cramped student house I called home for a year during university. Together, my housemates and I dug and planted the garden on impulse with an appalling lack of knowledge between us—intuition and guesswork served as our guide. Sure, I lost a lot of plants to rookie mistakes and neglect but to my surprise (and luck) I was able to harvest and enjoy more fresh, organically grown beans, tomatoes, lettuce, onions, carrots, and potatoes than I could even eat, all on a meager student budget.

Years later, and with a lot of gardening practice behind me, I am (thankfully) no longer as destitute as I was in my student days. Yet growing an organic food garden has evolved to become a far more important priority than just putting good food in my belly during tough times. Over time I have cultivated—or rather my gardens have cultivated in me—the knowledge, self-sufficiency, and confidence to stave off full dependency on the supermarket and to live rich in homegrown goodness throughout the year. My own little urban rooftop farm has reignited my childlike sense of wonder about the world and a depth of pride and excitement that lasts through every step of the growing process.

▲

Balcony railing boxes make an unlikely, but surprisingly bountiful micro-farm. This one is bursting with tomatoes and peppers galore!

I haven't had a backyard since that student house, but I have had many gardens both in-ground and above, and all because Scylla's resourcefulness, ingenuity, and disregard for North American social norms invited me to rethink my own limitations and turn them into advantages.

Many urban dwellers suffer from an incapacitating anxiety complex about space. We've gotten it into our heads that either we need to own land or we need lots of it in order to grow food. And if it's not a lack of space it's the wrong type. Barring those problems it's a lack of knowledge, money, or . . . There is always something that keeps us from giving it a go.

It is true that behind every sweet, organically grown tomato and leafy bundle of fresh basil is a healthy, happy garden. What's not true is the idea that you have to have a backyard, a country farm, or an encyclopedic knowledge of crop growing under your belt to make a healthy food garden happen. Right now, all over the world, urban gardeners are successfully contributing to local food economies in inspiring ways. In Havana, Cuba, a reported 50 to 80 percent of the city's fresh produce is grown in urban gardens—all of it organically grown! The only thing stopping us from following their example as small-space farmers is us.

I'm not going to lie to you. There *is* a heck of a lot to learn when it comes to growing a food garden. But you don't need to know everything now in order to begin. You'll learn over time through doing, succeeding, and yes, even failing. To become a food gardener, you need only a little direction (this book) and a plant or two to begin with. Expanding from there, your experience and confidence will grow along with your garden. And most important, remember this: without a doubt, you will make mistakes. All gardeners do from time to time, even the experienced ones. Grant yourself permission to learn through messing up, and before you know it you'll find yourself with bowls of ripe strawberries, bundles of fresh herbs, the perfect tomato sandwich, and your own fantasy food garden.

This suburbanite dug up the front lawn and put in a veggie patch, complete with a brightly painted cold frame in which to grow mustard greens, and a rain barrel that collects water from the roof.

Going and Growing Organic

Recently, the question of what is going into our food and where it comes from has spun a booming cultural shift toward organics that shows no signs of stopping. Many of us have transitioned to buying locally grown, seasonal food that does not have to travel thousands of miles to our table. We are also considering the cost and quality of the food we eat from an environmental and personal health standpoint. If you are reading this book, chances are you have already considered these questions and are hoping to bring more organic food to your table, affordably. But with so many buzzwords flying around, you are probably wondering more than ever: just what does organic gardening mean for you and your garden?

Simply put, organic gardening is achieved without chemicals or pesticides. If you're avoiding both, you're most of the way there. It is also about looking to nature as a guide in building a healthy, balanced garden. Your goal as an organic gardener isn't to create a perfect, micromanaged world where pests and diseases don't exist. Far from it! Organic gardening treats the soil as a living entity that must be supported and fed. In turn, healthy soil nourishes healthy plants that are up to the task of defending themselves against the problems that will inevitably arise. Using chemicals has the opposite effect. It gives the plants a quick short-term hit, but kills soil organisms and just about every other living critter along the way.

In that sense organic gardening is not nearly as difficult or intimidating as it is sometimes thought to be. Most of us aren't managing a 10-acre family farm—it's a lot easier to keep on top of problems on a 6' × 4' condo balcony where slugs and snails aren't an issue. Even on the ground, where slugs reign supreme, organic gardening can actually save work over the long haul because it is primarily about prevention. And with no unrealistic ideas about perfection to aspire to, there's more time to kick your feet up and enjoy the delicious, and completely chemical-free fruit of your labor!

Getting Started

Section 1, "Good Growing: An Edible Gardening Primer," is designed to inspire you to create your own miniature organic farm regardless of whether your space is ideal or far from it. These chapters cover the groundwork critical to taking the first steps in assessing what you've got and transforming it into a working garden, and this section will also provide the know-how you'll need to face future challenges that are par for the course in any garden.

Knowing how to get a garden started is one thing; understanding the needs of each plant is another. Treat Section 2, "The Plants," as a helping hand—a place to begin exploring and understanding the care requirements and specific growing needs of an assortment of delicious produce. Get excited about fascinating and otherworldly heirloom varieties that are as beautiful as they are tasty. Follow tips and tricks geared to container and in-ground gardeners. Take another look whenever you get stuck and need help with a crop or when you decide to start growing a new plant.

Each of the three chapters in Section 2—"Vegetables," "Fruit," and "Herbs and Edible Flowers"—is organized alphabetically, with some plants grouped together based on family or growing similarities. A general growing outline appears at the beginning of each group of mixed entries, followed by the specific growing needs and harvesting tips for each plant.

The hardcore harvest season may happen a little before or after late summer in your region, but it all amounts to the same thing: *mega-awesome bounty*. Possibly even *too* much of it. Losing any of that hard-won booty to rot would be a crying shame. You've got the growing part down, but how do you know when to harvest a tomato or cucumber? And what exactly does a successful gardener do with a tsunami of tomatoes and legions of hot peppers? Section 2 offers advice on when and how to harvest specific crops; look to Section 3, "Reaping the Harvest," for general harvesting tips such as the best time of day and how often to pick.

Section 3 is also the place to go to learn about old-school and new-school storage and preservation techniques. With a little know-how and a couple of hours on a Sunday afternoon, you can make the rewards of the season last for months to come.

About the Projects and Recipes

The ingredients I have used in the recipes reflect how my family eats: Whole-grain rice and flours, real organic butter and dairy, and baked goods that are low in sugar, with maple syrup, honey, or agave syrup in the place of the granulated stuff. I adjusted some of my tried-and-true recipes to reflect a more mainstream taste for sweetness, but if you need more, by all means go for it! The flavors of ingredients shift depending on location, soil, and even the weather—don't be afraid to make tweaks that suit your own tastes and eating habits.

All projects in this book have been rated with a difficulty scale from the easiest to the most difficult so you can see at a glance which projects are right for you.

Good Growing:
An Edible Gardening Primer

CHAPTER 1:

Growing Anywhere and Everywhere

Your patio, balcony, rooftop, deck, sidewalk median, tree pit, planter box, or window ledge is a potential garden waiting to happen.

During the Great Depression, World War II, and other times when food and money have been tight, people all over North America planted seeds in the soil and grew green beans or tomatoes without thinking twice about it. No one worried about whether his or her space was the "right" space. This everyday attitude toward food gardening still exists in lots of other countries around the world, but through time and a bit of backward thinking we've come to believe that a garden—especially one that produces food—requires a mythical perfect space. This perfect space is generally thought to be in the ground. Preferably in a backyard. Most likely stuck way in the back where no one can see it.

I'll admit that there are days when I dream of having a yard of my own that I can turn into my own private mini farm. But then I look around at my sunny, thriving rooftop container garden and my not-so-shabby community garden plot and realize I'm doing all right. My gardens may not be a rectangle in the back corner of a sprawling lot. And okay, they're located blocks away from each other, yet it turns out that they are adequate. More than adequate, in fact. I see and sample the evidence on my table every day.

The good news is that plants want to grow. Some will take up residence in the most oppressive conditions. Most of the plants we've domesticated tend to be a bit pickier than your average sidewalk weed, but plenty of herbs and veggies have the tenacity and audacity to thrive in some fairly surprising places. If a front yard is all you've got, then why not replace the lawn with a raised-bed food farm? That lawn was a useless pain in the butt anyway. What about that square of dirt behind the garage? Who says you've got to plant that strip separating your front walkway from the neighbor's with hedges? Why not fill it with Swiss chard? Or purple basil? Or an incredible crop of lavender! Some of the most unexpected places have the best light and conditions for growing coveted sun-loving food crops. That "perfect" site could be sitting right underneath your nose.

Even the most space-deprived would-be gardener can grow sprouts in a dark kitchen or a window box of microgreens (see "No-Space Grub," page 14) or a pot of chives on a window ledge (see "Windowsill Edibles," page 16). These may seem small, but they are a start that could lead to more ambitious goals and the pursuit of space beyond the windowsill. Today a tomato plant on the fire escape, tomorrow you're poring through seed catalogs with a highlighter and a wild look in your eyes.

I found this tiny cobbled-together, raised-bed tomato patch tucked behind a garage in a Toronto alley. While it is not aesthetically the sort of garden many would aspire to, it continues to serve as an inspiration to me and a reminder to measure my success as a food gardener on my own terms. If this gardener can make a go of it in the very worst of conditions, anyone can!

No-Space Grub

Regardless of space or lighting conditions, anyone, and I mean anyone, can grow fresh sprouts in the kitchen. Sprouts are chockablock full of all kinds of good stuff, including antioxidants, enzymes, vitamin C, fiber, and protein, adding a nutrition-packed zing to soups, salads, and sandwiches.

If you've got just a little bit of light and a windowsill, try your hand at growing a mix of microgreens. These Lilliputian young seedlings are essentially sprouts that have been left to develop just a little longer—sometimes up to a week or more after sprouting. The difference is not just a matter of age but also of flavor, color, and texture. These days microgreens are all the rage as garnishes in finer restaurants, but you can grow your own for pennies. See the "Resources" section at the end of the book for premixed packets or mix up your own using the following suggestions.

All kinds of seeds, from the tiniest ones to larger beans, can be sprouted in soil. Health food and bulk food stores are great places to find affordable seeds for sprouting. Choose seed that has not been treated with a fungicide; check first or buy "certified organic."

YOU WILL NEED

- Seeds or beans to sprout
- Window box or container with drainage holes (minimum 4" deep)
- Potting soil
- Drainage tray without holes to catch water

TRY SPROUTING THESE SEEDS:

Earthy Sprouts
lettuce, spinach, sunflower, green pea, adzuki bean, broccoli, lentil, alfalfa, beet, cabbage

Spicy Sprouts
mustard, cress, daikon, radish, onion, kale, arugula

Juicing Sprouts
wheatgrass, alfalfa, mung bean

1. To hasten germination, soak the seeds in room temperature water for 4–8 hours. Soak hard-shelled beans longer than small seeds.

2. Drain the water and give the seeds a quick rinse.

3. Fill your container three-quarters full with premoistened potting soil. Spread the soil out evenly, but don't worry about making it perfectly level. A few bumps in the road won't hurt a bit.

4. Spread the seed evenly on top of the soil and cover with a thin blanket of moist soil. See page 25 for further information about sowing seeds.

5. Place the container on top of the drainage tray and water lightly. Set your growing station in a warm location and keep the soil moist like a damp sponge. Your seeds won't require light until they've germinated. Germination times differ depending on the seed. Radish, cress, cabbage, and mustard take about 4–8 days; sunflower and onion can take as long as 10–14 days.

6. When the little seedlings begin to poke their way through the soil surface, move the whole kit and caboodle to a sunny windowsill. Remember to keep the soil moist, not soaking.

To Harvest: Start harvesting sprouts shortly after germination. Simply cut the young 'uns off at the soil line with a pair of scissors as needed. Wait another few days to two weeks before harvesting microgreens (seedlings with four or more sets of leaves).

After Harvest: Continue cutting sprouts and microgreens until the harvest stops. Wheatgrass will produce more than one crop from the same planting. Compost the roots and soil and start again (page 46).

Free 'n' Easy: Rather than buying new plastic containers, grow your plants in recycled margarine, yogurt, and takeout containers. Poke a few holes in the bottom for drainage, place the lid underneath as a drip tray, and you're good to go.

Hydroponic Sprouting: Ye olde familiar Mason jar method of sprouting has fallen out of favor in recent times because of highly publicized salmonella and *E. coli* scares. The truth is that though this classic technique seems easy, keeping bacteria and mold from growing alongside your greens is a bit of a juggling act. On the other hand, growing sprouts in a tray of soil is foolproof and safe.

Windowsill Edibles

A wide assortment of herbs, greens, lettuces, edible flowers, and even chili peppers will produce better than expected on a sunny windowsill, especially during the summer months when the days are longer and the light is more intense. In the absence of a sunny window you're going to need a little help in the way of an artificial grow light, but even that can be as simple as a full-spectrum bulb in a cheap shop light.

GENERAL CARE

Chances are that your windowsill garden isn't going to stay alive forever, even indoors. To keep plants happy for the longest time possible, be sure they are getting good drainage, ample water, and as much light as possible. Water when the soil has gone from damp like a sponge to slightly dry within an inch of the top. How often you need to water depends on the location, because pots set on a hot and sunny window situated above an electric baseboard heater are likely to dry quickly, whereas those set in a north-facing window with a draft may retain moisture for up to a week. Always sample the soil moisture an inch or so below the surface with your finger before pouring on more water.

Increase the humidity around the leaves during the dry months by setting pots on top of a tray of pebbles or spritzing the air with a water bottle.

PEST PREVENTION AND MAINTENANCE

Hold back on fertilizers during the slow-growing winter months. With short days and little sun, plants will grow leggy and fragile. Cut your plants back regularly to encourage stocky, bushy growth.

CHOOSING PLANTS

When growing in a mixed pot or window box, choose plants with similar needs. Mediterranean herbs such as oregano, marjoram, sage, and thyme that love lots of sun and good drainage are a guaranteed mix. Lettuce greens also grow well together, but it's best to give hot peppers their own pot.

For indoor growing, most herbs are easiest and fastest if started from transplants. Basil, calendula, violas, pansies, and coriander are the exception, growing to an edible size quickly from seed. When it comes to leafy greens and lettuce, seeds are the only way to go.

CHOOSING CONTAINERS

Window boxes are the obvious choice because their thin, boxy shape is tailor-made for windowsills. However, there are all kinds of fashionable options these days, including individual square pots like the one depicted. Window boxes and pots should be a minimum of 5" deep with drainage holes and water-catching trays that fit neatly underneath. The deeper the pot, the better your bet for keeping the plants healthy over the long term. Containers without holes can be adjusted with the addition of an inch or two of gravel or broken pot shards placed at the bottom as a water reservoir. This method will work over the short term but requires some restraint when watering to avoid drowning the plants.

1. Fill your container or window box with moistened potting soil to within about 3" of the top.

2. If planting transplants or cuttings, make a hole for each plant by pushing some soil off to the sides.

3. Remove transplants from their current pots and place them in position in the new container or window box. Try to leave some space between plants for roots to spread and grow. In general, no more than three plants should go in a 12" × 6" window box.

4. Once placed, fill in the spaces around the plants, making sure that the crown (where the roots meet the stem) is not buried underneath the soil surface. An inch or two of space should be left between the soil surface and the top of the container to allow for watering.

5. Water everything in until the soil is wet right through to the bottom of the pot.

YOU WILL NEED

- Window box or pot with drainage holes
- Pot shards or rocks (optional)
- Potting soil
- Seeds, transplants (small plants), or rooted cuttings

SUPER SUNNY WINDOWS

- Thyme
- Oregano
- Sage
- Marjoram
- Chili peppers (try super tiny 'Chinese Ornamental' or vigorous 'Red Rocoto')
- Basil (try compact varieties like 'Purple Bush')
- Parsley
- Cress
- Calendula

SLIGHTLY SHADY WINDOWS

- Mint
- Chives
- Lettuce
- Spinach
- Parsley
- Thyme
- Mizuna
- Miner's lettuce aka Claytonia
- Viola and pansy

Finding Space

So what do you do if you've got ambitions beyond the windowsill but not a scrap of outdoor space to your name? Why not borrow some? These days, a growing number of community garden organizations are spreading the love of growing food.

Growing Communities

By establishing space in public parks, on private land, and in former waste spaces, they offer locals a chance to take up a trowel alongside their neighbors. Each garden is as distinctive as the groups that plant it, with their own model and rules. Some assign small tracts of land or "plots" to individuals; others are a joint venture, with a group tending a space collectively. A community or allotment garden can be as small as a couple of plots or as large as an entire city block with hundreds of members. Tour the gardens near you and find one that suits your needs and style. If finding a spot is a no-go in your area, consider starting one with eager neighbors. Check out the "Resources" section at the end of the book for books and websites that will guide you through the logistics of getting a community garden off the ground.

Takin' It to the Streets

Guerrilla gardening is the mother of community gardening, or perhaps more aptly put, its defiant, rebellious cousin. Guerrilla gardening is about gardening anywhere and everywhere with neither attachment nor permission. Most guerrilla gardeners garden in a drive-by fashion, dropping in seeds and plants without ever returning to tend or nurture the site.

But is it possible to grow food within those parameters? After all, growing food is primarily an act of cultivation that requires commitment, and more often than not, the expectation of a future harvest. Some guerrilla gardeners choose to invest some time into the space, returning regularly to care for the plants as they would a community garden or backyard farm. Others choose plants that will thrive unassisted and produce food for the public to enjoy. Determining what will grow unaided in your area depends a lot on your climate and growing conditions. For example, residents of San Francisco know all too well that edibles like nasturtiums, blackberries, and fennel will thrive in fallow lots and fields in their city without a scrap of human intervention. Unfortunately, the plants that bloom best also tend to be invasive opportunists, crowding out native growth (and everything else, for that matter) if left to their own devices. When starting a guerrilla garden, consider the long-term effects of your actions and aim to spread some edible goodwill rather than cause damage.

Dreaming and Scheming

For decades vegetable gardening was wrongly perceived as a low-class, entirely practical, but unsightly subset of the gardening world. Inedible flowers and ornamentals were proudly displayed out front, while the vegetable garden was shoved into a sunny, but very much hidden, back corner.

Making Food Fabulous

Fortunately our attitudes are radically shifting thanks to a newfound enthusiasm for old-fashioned heirloom plants, many of which happen to be colorful and gorgeous. Suddenly the once lowly Swiss chard and overlooked old kale are getting the respect and attention they deserve. Gardeners are bringing edible plants into the spotlight, tossing out those stifling old assumptions and allowing these plants to share space in the hallowed flower bed. What's more, we are also seeing a new appreciation for flowers as food. Many of them make a tasty, nutritious, and eye-pleasing addition to the dinner or dessert plate. Small-space gardeners no longer have to choose between beauty and practicality. We can enjoy our flowers and eat them too!

Adding Edibles to a Garden

Designing a stylish edible landscape can be as easy as tucking a couple of sculptural veggies among the bedding plants where an ornamental grass or leafy heuchera used to steal the show. Big and bold foliage plants such as 'Rhubarb' Swiss chard and 'Redbor' kale can keep pace with hostas and coleus for the duration of the growing season, while tall, lacy, and delicate dill and metallic 'Bronze Fennel' make a great replacement for inedible cow parsley and astilbe.

Swapping out expensive ornamentals for their edible lookalikes saves cash too. Artichokes are a type of thistle, growing as fantastically architectural as any ornamental thistle but rivaling them with a gourmet delicacy at their cycle's end. Leave your average leek in the ground over winter and it will send up a colorful, globular flower the following year—a thrifty and edible version of the overpriced ornamental onion (*Allium giganteum*). Purple shiso and 'Dark Opal' basil glow in a sunny spot with the added bonus that you can harvest the leaves for tasty tea and pesto. Try variegated varieties of typically average plants such as 'Variegata' hot peppers, 'Variegata' strawberry (*Fragaria vesca*), or 'Alaska Mix' nasturtium. There is even a variegated white-and-green tomato plant. The tomatoes are your run-of-the-mill red, but the plant is outstanding!

Clockwise from top left: Majestic amaranth and Swiss chard decorate a sunny boulevard; strawberries, violas, and 'Purple Ruffles' basil share a springtime strawberry jar; colorful beans beautify a fence; a pea trellis can be built from tree prunings; stunning 'Purple Ruffles' basil.

The Contemporary Potager

Simply tucking ornamental edibles into a flower bed is only the beginning. If you're into planning, decorating, and organizing you'll have a field day designing an entirely ornamental kitchen garden or potager. Although potagers were by tradition obsessive-compulsive in their dedication to a formal, boxy arrangement, there is no reason why you can't plant in loose groupings, drifts, or spirals. Organizing your plants into cooperative groupings, aka companion planting (page 34), doesn't just look good, it's also smart design that benefits the overall health of the garden.

Border the perimeter of your garden with eye-catching, low-growing and colorful lettuces, nasturtiums, chamomile, thyme, strawberries, curly leaf parsley, or violas. Take your cue from the formal kitchen garden by boxing in squares with neatly trimmed edible hedges of rosemary, lavender, or blueberries.

Consider growing upward as well as out. Create arrangements around a tall focal point such as a wooden trellis or bamboo tripod covered in tall runner beans, peas, or tomatoes. Erect an organically shaped sculpture from foraged branches and tough twine. Underplant with lettuce, thyme, or 'Purple Ruffles' basil, an arrangement that both shields the soil and blocks out weeds, making your job that much easier down the line.

Vertically grown edibles increase productivity in a smaller space and can magically disguise drab fences and create privacy between neighbors. Plant tough and pest-resistant go-getters like 'Mexican Sour Gherkin' (*Melothria scabra*), a cucumber relative that bears delicate foliage and adorable little fruit, or 'Scarlet Runner Bean,' whose vibrant blooms turn into big, pendulous pods. A row of Jerusalem artichokes makes an easy-to-grow living screen with sunflower-like flowers perched high atop 10-foot-tall stems. Trail a hops vine (*Humulus lupulus*) up a pole or along a fence for fast and easy coverage. Harvest the flowers for home-brewed beer or herbal tea; steam young shoots in the spring as you would asparagus. Hops take their cue from bindweed, growing aggressively and wildly—once this plant is in you'll never be rid of it. Grow it in large containers to prevent spreading.

These hot pink tuberous begonia flowers are ▶
practically fluorescent in a pot. And they're
edible too! The juicy petals are as sour as
lemons and make a convincing substitute.

CHAPTER 2:

Gotta Get Plants

It goes without saying that your garden needs plants. Buying ready-to-go potted transplants is the obvious choice, but it can be a distressingly expensive way to fill up the bare earth of a brand-new garden.

Fortunately there are other ways to get plants that don't cost a penny. Many gardeners have a surplus of seeds and seedlings and are happy to share. Go online to find communities to trade with, or try splitting orders between friends—small-space gardeners rarely need more than a few seeds from each pack, and some small plants can be cut up into more plants (see page 31).

When making purchases, farmer's markets, yard sales, horticultural societies, ethnic food stores, Chinatown sidewalk stalls, garden shows, and even specialty food markets are all great places to find unusual transplants and seeds at reduced prices.

The best way to expand your collection is through seed growing, because seeds can be easily and affordably shipped through the mail. Even the best varieties are only a few bucks a pack, amounting to less than a quarter for a tomato plant and a fraction of a penny per head of lettuce. Thousands of seed companies cater to a multitude of botanical desires, and many offer full-color catalogs online. Shopping this way saves paper even if it does mean missing out on the age-old tradition of flipping pages and highlighting favorites while soaking in the tub.

Making Plants: Growing from Seed

In the store, seeds come with words like *open-pollinated*, *heirloom*, and *hybrid* on the label. Open-pollinated and heirloom varieties are those that have developed through natural pollination, while heirlooms are the old-fashioned types that have been passed down for generations. Scoop the seeds from a single pepper, tomato, or melon come fall and you'll have enough to grow next year for yourself and the entire neighborhood. Hybrids are specially bred, typically for disease and insect resistance. They are a good choice when growing plants that are especially prone to these problems in your region. Unfortunately, they produce sterile seeds, a fact that will keep you dependent on "the man" forever.

What You Need

You can start seeds in just about anything that can hold soil and that drains out the bottom. The best place to look for equipment is in the recycling bin, and not the garden department. Don't waste your hard-earned money on those plastic greenhouses. Reuse small plastic containers with a few holes poked into the bottom. Put the lid underneath and you've got an instant drip tray! Sow a flat of lettuce or onion seeds in those plastic containers store-bought greens come in. Cut a plastic bottle in half and invert the funnel-shaped top into the bottom half and you've got a handy self-watering seed starter.

The early life of a seedling is vital to the long-term health of the plant. Growing seedlings indoors makes them more susceptible to disease than their direct-sown siblings. The health of young plants rests firmly on a foundation of light and airy, water-retentive yet well-draining soil specially prepared for starting seeds.

Don't forget to label your containers as soon as you sow the seeds, or you'll end up with a grab bag of anonymous plants come planting time. Different plants are easy enough to identify, but most varieties look alike. I devise miniature flags from strips of self-stick paper folded over toothpicks. Tongue depressors and Popsicle sticks are attractive in small pots and can be color-coded for at-a-glance identification.

Sowing and Planting

How and when to get seeds started differs depending on the plant. Some should be planted indoors as long as 3 months before the last frost date, while others can be sown outdoors as soon as the soil thaws in the spring. The exact length of time for each plant is too much to memorize. Stay on top of the start dates with a Seed Starting and Planting Chart (page 202) that calculates when to get each crop started and when to get it into the ground. Hang the chart in a convenient spot where you'll be reminded of approaching dates. It may seem like a hassle to fill out now, but it will save you a lot of confused scrambling later on.

Lots of plants such as peas, lettuce, leafy greens, and beans grow best when sown outside directly into the spot where they will live out their lives, whether straight into a garden bed or in a pot. Direct sowing has all the benefits of starting from seed without the hassle of finding space in the bedroom or kitchen for pots of baby plants. See Section 2 of this book to find out when to sow specific plants.

Seeds must also be sown at different depths depending on the plant, although you can pretty much count on the general rule that seeds should be covered to a depth roughly equal to their longest side. This means that very tiny seeds are sown on the surface with hardly any soil on top, and larger seeds are sown into a hole dug to roughly double their size. Easy, right? If you find yourself stumped when the moment comes, no worries; most seed packets will tell you exactly what to do.

To sow indoor seeds, fill your container to within ½" or so of the top with premoistened seed starting mix and tamp it down a bit with your fingers or a similarly sized pot. If the holes in your pot seem too big to hold loose soil, stick a little piece of newspaper in the bottom beforehand. Sow seeds to the depth required for each plant, adding a maximum of two seeds to a 4" pot. When sowing large trays or direct-sowing outdoors, follow the instructions on the seed packet for the most ideal spacing and distribute the seeds as evenly as possible. Place pots and trays in a warm spot and keep the soil damp, like a wrung-out sponge, while the seeds germinate. Germination times depend on the plant, so don't freak if you don't find little babies poking up right away.

Toilet Roll Seed-Starting Cells

Skip the peat pellets and compressed pots. They look cool, but they're a pain in the butt and a waste of money. A bag of seed-starting mix and a handful of toilet roll tubes are a good green option that carries all the benefits of a peat pellet but costs pennies a plant. These are especially great for starting beans and sunflower seeds, which dislike having their roots disrupted during transplanting.

1. Stand up three, five, or seven toilet rolls on a plate or tray and arrange them into a circular grouping.

2. Loosely tie a piece of twine around the group to hold them in place.

3. Gently pack each tube with premoistened seed-starting soil, lightly tamping it in until it is near the top.

4. Plant a single seed in each tube at the appropriate depth and water it lightly.

5. When the seedling is ready to plant outside, gently tease off the outer layer of paper, leaving a thin layer of paper intact before planting each tube in its own hole.

Growing Up Baby

If you're using a humidity dome or cover, remove it as soon as little plants begin to poke up through the soil. Everyone knows that seedlings need water and light to survive, but few consider a third requirement: air circulation.

Ventilation is rarely a problem outdoors, but our sealed-up winter homes tend to have still and stale air, the perfect breeding ground for diseases such as damping off (page 73) that prey on vulnerable young plants. If you can set a small electric fan near the growing seedlings, this will help.

Newly germinated seeds must also receive light immediately—at least 12–16 hours a day with fluorescent lights hung no more than 2–4" above the leaves at all times. Yep, that close. Anything more and seedlings tend to grow tall, thin, and unhealthy as they stretch toward weak light. A south-facing windowsill is okay in a pinch, but usually chilly and not quite bright enough. Invest in a cheap shop light that holds two tubes, one cool white and one warm white, and suspend the box above your plants on a hanging chain. Alternatively, set the plants on top of a stack of phone books or bricks, removing a layer as the seedlings grow.

Newly germinated plants are just like chicken eggs in that they carry all the nutrition they require with them in the form of *seed leaves*, the first leaves that emerge from the soil. Those are soon replaced by a second set, known as the *true leaves*. Seedlings start to require some added nutrition once the seed leaves shrivel off and disappear. Some seed-starting soil mixes come with a bit of organic matter in them, but if yours doesn't, now is the time to add a teaspoon of vermicompost and sea kelp (page 65) for good measure.

Inevitably, more seeds are bound to germinate than anticipated. When that happens, you'll need to practice some tough love by thinning out tightly packed seedlings while they are still small so the plants have room to expand. It's a brutal job—even I have a tough time doing it, my impulse being to simply dig the extras out and transplant them elsewhere. Don't. You'll only risk damaging the delicate root system of all the plants in an effort to save a few. Instead, snip the extras off at the soil line with a pair of scissors. The culled tender seedlings of Swiss chard, kale, leafy greens, beets, carrots, and onions are a tasty addition to salads. Don't see it as wasting plants; think of it as getting an early harvest!

◀ Clockwise from top left: Onion seedlings ready to transplant; this tomato plant has sustained cold and sun damage because it was not properly hardened off; don't forget to add tags; tongue depressors sprayed with chalkboard paint make cheap tags.

Moving Them Out

The right time to shift your seedlings from their cozy home indoors to the big bad world outside depends on the individual needs of each plant. Many can go out as soon as the frost-free date is reached in your area, but some should go out before and some after. Check the care instructions for each plant.

All transplants that have been grown indoors must go through a process called *hardening off*, a system of acclimating plants and transitioning them from a cushy life indoors to the harsh outside elements. Planting them directly in the soil outdoors would send tender plants into a state of shock and kill them off quickly. There goes all of your hard work into the compost bin.

1. When the temperatures have warmed enough, set your little seedlings outside in a sheltered spot for short periods of time every day.

2. Gradually increase their stint outdoors over the course of 2 weeks.

3. Slowly move sun-loving plants out of the shade until they've grown accustomed to the intensity of outdoor light.

Handling young seedlings: Always hold them by the leaves rather than the stems. Damaged leaves can grow back; seedlings with a damaged stem are done for.

Cleaning Pots: Once you've transferred your transplants outside, save the pots and use them again and again. Soak them in hot, soapy water with a few capfuls of hydrogen peroxide (aka oxygenated bleach) and/or vinegar, and they'll be clean and sterile for the next crop.

Making More Plants

Creating new plants from cuttings always makes me feel like I'm up to something disobedient and defiant. How can such a cheap and easy way to multiply your harvest not be a little wicked?

Plants such as mint, basil, scented geranium, lavender, thyme, rosemary, lemon verbena, and oregano are particularly easy to root. Using a pair of scissors, make an angled cut from a shoot just below the spot where a leaf is attached. Stick stems in a jar of water and you'll see roots in less than a week. Make arrangements to share cuttings with a group of gardening friends and you can all reap big-time benefits from just a couple of plants.

CHAPTER 3:

Get This Party Started Right

The first thing to do before starting any garden is to consider the space. I know, not exciting, right? You're itching to order up a ton of seeds and get your hands in some dirt right now!

Taking the time to consider the space you've got can feel like a drag, especially when the conclusion doesn't jibe with your fantasy garden. However, understanding how factors like sun, soil, and exposure affect your space can mean the difference between a garden that thrives and one that works only on paper.

Making realistic plans will help you realize limitations and maximize your assets. Instead of imagining the worst, think of the unexpected directions your garden can take when you have a little clarity working in your favor.

Exposure

Vegetable gardens generally do best in a spot that receives *full sun*. Earnest gardeners often dupe themselves into believing that the weak light underneath a tree or a north-facing windowsill qualifies. Unfortunately, it doesn't. If you've got shade, you need to call it like it is now and spare yourself the disappointment. Almost no edibles thrive in deep shade. Happily, *partial shade* will support an array of leafy vegetables and herbs, although in some cases the reduced sun can result in slightly lower yields. To get an accurate gauge, observe the light throughout the day and watch how it changes with the seasons. A south-facing direction, though often considered the best, can be thwarted by a high fence, a tall building, or a bank of trees whose leaves have just come in for the summer. Try to situate permanent beds and containers in a direction that makes the best use of available light, especially early in the day when the light is most intense.

UNDERSTANDING LIGHT

Full Sun: 6 hours or more of direct sun per day.
Partial Shade: 4–6 hours of direct sun per day.

Airflow and wind are another consideration that falls under exposure. Food gardens thrive inside a windbreak where there is protection from strong, damaging winds. Imagine how it feels when a gentle breeze dances across your skin. Now imagine a strong wind pummeling

you in the face. It's not so different for plants. A light breeze moving through the garden reduces stagnation and regulates temperature. High winds, on the other hand, can funnel between buildings and thwack your plants head-on, quickly drying out the soil, knocking over containers, and breaking limbs. Trees, bushes, tall plants, and walls all act as windbreaks on the ground level, but plants on roofs and high-rise balconies are often more susceptible without natural blocks up there in the sky. The trick is to create light windbreaks that disrupt the flow but don't stop the wind entirely. Secure a latticed trellis or open-weave fence in place and group your plants in clusters, with vulnerable plants placed in the front and the toughest in the back and closest to the trellis, where they can provide additional protection.

Buildings, walls, and tall trees can direct airflow, and they can also have a hand in creating pockets of shade or heat within a small area. All kinds of factors, including vehicles, ponds, sidewalks, brick, and fences, can collude to create differing microclimates within the same space. A heat-absorbing brick wall creates a cozy backdrop for cucumbers or tomatoes. Relocate a pot of leafy greens underneath the cooling shelter of a balcony overhang to extend the harvest into the dog days of summer. Microclimates can really work in your favor if you take the time to understand how they are at play within your space.

GROW AN EDIBLE WINDBREAK

- Artichokes
- Blackberries
- Blueberries
- Corn
- Jerusalem artichokes
- Kale
- Raspberries
- Rosemary
- Runner beans
- Swiss chard

Making Arrangements: How, Where, and When

The way you position your plants in the garden, whether a container garden or an in-ground one, is almost as important as its location or when you sow them. Plants that are spaced too close are forced to compete for root space, nutrients, and moisture. The leaves start to overlap and shade each other, raising the humidity around them and eventually creating an environment that welcomes disease. On the other hand, spacing plants too far apart is not as innocuous as it may seem. Productivity is obviously lower because the less you grow, the less you get. A little shading is actually good—it cools the soil slightly and keeps it moist longer. Better for the environment and less work for you!

Growing your plants in groupings, rather than rows, is an unbeatable way to pack more into a tight space without causing a ruckus. Visualize your garden as a chessboard and place plants in staggered groupings of 3–2–3 or 2–3–2, like this:

Won't You Be My Neighbor? Companion Planting

Companion planting is sort of like planning the seating chart for a wedding. I'm not going to lie; it can also be as irritating. Unless you're looking for ringside seats to a fight, best not to stick your Jesus-loving uncle Bill next to your abortion doctor sister-in-law, Phyllis. But companion planting isn't all about playing the diplomat; it's also a way to get plant communities working together cooperatively to help create a thriving ecosystem. The good news is that companion planting doesn't just work when plants are sharing the same soil. Even container gardeners can reap some of the cooperative benefits by placing pots of partner plants next to or nearby their pals.

There Goes the Neighborhood: Rotating Crops

Crop rotation is akin to playing a long-term game of musical chairs in the garden. Every plant is different, inviting specific pests and diseases and demanding more of certain nutrients than others. Growing the same crop in the same spot year after year drains the soil in the same way that printing a color image with a lot of red in it exhausts the red cartridge while the others stay full. In the garden, that kind of lopsided bleed-out can lead to sick plants. To make matters worse, some diseases and pests can end up taking residence in the soil around the plants they prey on most. Keeping those plants in the same place is like inviting pests to an all-you-can-eat buffet where their favorite meal is served every day.

Noting where you grow each crop allows you to perform the old switcheroo, confusing pests and diseases and giving the soil a chance to play catch-up on depleted nutrients. It's not always easy to know which should follow which, but as a general rule, replacing a crop with a member of a different family will make a big difference. Section 2 of this book identifies the plant families each crop belongs to and provides tips on the best swaps to keep things copacetic.

TYPES OF COMPANIONS

Opposites Attract: Planting light feeders with heavy feeders, and deep-rooted plants with shallow-rooted plants, makes the best use of soil nutrition and prevents competition. Deep-rooted plants dig up the soil and bring nutrition from way below up to the top, while shallow-rooted plants create a web of roots near the surface, preventing erosion.

Pest Repellents: Some insect pests are put off by the smell or chemical composition of certain plants. Protect vulnerable plants by growing repellent plants nearby. Surrounding a vulnerable plant with something strong-smelling like onion or garlic can also confuse pests. **TRY:** marigolds, garlic, garlic chives, onions, catnip, lavender, mint, and coriander.

The Popular Crowd: The flowers of some plants attract beneficial parasitic wasps, bees, butterflies, and other pollinators to the garden, keeping insect pest populations in check and ensuring that crops are pollinated. **TRY:** borage, mint, dill, yarrow, calendula, and basil. For more information, see page 75.

Trap Plants: Insect pests are known to prefer some plants over others. Exploit this preference by growing a known pest magnet nearby your favorite crop as a decoy. Once infested, remove the decoy and destroy it, pests and all. **TRY:** nasturtiums and mustard greens.

Feeder Plants: Legumes such as beans and peas can convert nitrogen from the air and release it into the soil. Follow legumes with nitrogen-loving brassicas such as broccoli, cabbage, or kale.

Shelter from the Storm: Grow tall and sturdy plants in front of delicate and sensitive crops as a protective shield against wind or excess heat.

Flavor Enhancers: Although it hasn't been officially proven, some plants are said to boost and even alter the flavor of their companions. **TRY:** borage with strawberry, chervil with radishes, bee balm with tomatoes.

Underplanting: Grow short, quick-growing, and shallow-rooted plants such as lettuce greens below tall leafy plants like tomatoes or okra. The short plants will shade the soil surface for the tall plants while they work to get established, and the tall plants will provide shade coverage for the short plants later in the season when the summer heats up. **TRY:** leafy greens, lettuce, Mexican marigold (*Tagetes minuta*), parsley, and thyme.

◀ Clockwise from top left: Plant nectar-rich flowers that attract beneficial insects to the garden. Immature hover flies devour aphids; bumble bees are popular pollinators; lady beetle larvae are voracious aphid eaters; yellow jacket wasps are good general predators.

At the start of summer, replace mature lettuce growing underneath tomato plants with basil to keep the harvest coming. Even container gardeners can benefit from this growing strategy.

Second Sowings

Many of us tend to think of spring as the time to break out the seed collection and get to sowing, but spring is really only the beginning of several opportunities to get another crop growing. Depending on your climate, some seeds can be sown in the fall or as late as winter. Don't let the passing of spring call an end to your edible-garden dreams. Use these guidelines to get growing in almost any season.

Early to Midsummer Planting

Hot weather signals the end for many cool-season crops in most climates, regardless of proximity to the equator. When the peas are passing out and the lettuce is turning sappy and bitter, it's time to retire them to the compost heap and fill in the vacated spots with hot-weather plants. Rotating crops in this way makes the best use of prime garden real estate. **TRY:** direct-sown (see page 25) bush and pole beans, soy (edamame), corn, and lots and lots of basil.

Late-Summer Planting

Just as you counted the days until the last frost to determine spring planting times (see the Seed Starting and Planting Chart, page 202), the same method can be used to find out when to plant out cool crops before the growing season's last hurrah. Consult a *Farmer's Almanac* (www.almanac.com) to determine the first frost date for your area. Then look up the days to harvest for your desired crop in the Harvest Chart (see page 173). Count the listed number of days back from the first frost date to ascertain whether you've got enough time left in the season. Be sure to tack on an extra week or so to account for the shortening fall days. **TRY:** beans, carrots, peas, spinach, lettuce and greens, onions, pansies and violas, radicchio, cilantro, and radish.

Winter Crops

These plants can be sown again for a winter crop in frost-free and temperate zones. **TRY:** calendula, Swiss chard, greens, peas, kale, cabbage, pansies and violas, broccoli, turnips, and onions.

PLANTING TIPS AT A GLANCE

Whatcha Got? Identify the conditions in your space that will affect how your plants grow, including light and exposure, wind direction, microclimates (page 33), and soil type and fertility (page 42).

Location, Location, Location: Growing plants in staggered groupings instead of rows increases your harvest, cools the soil, locks moisture in longer, and allows them to work together communally. (See "Making Arrangements: How, Where, and When," page 34.)

Living with the Relatives: Following next year's crop in any given spot with plants from a different family gives the soil a much-needed rest and fools diseases and pests that may otherwise congregate in that area. (See "There Goes the Neighborhood: Rotating Crops," page 35.)

Thank You for Being a Friend: Position plants in cooperative groupings that increase the health of the whole (companion planting, page 34).

Out with the Old: Make prime use of space by replacing short-lived crops such as peas, radishes, and leafy greens with a follow-up crop, keeping the entire garden planted at all times. (See "Second Sowings," page 38.)

CHAPTER 4:

Different Strokes: Growing in the Ground and Growing in Containers

As you can imagine, when it comes to keeping plants in pots versus growing plants in the ground, there are some need-to-know differences. However, although some of the strategies and ingredients are different, in many ways the basic concepts are the same. For that reason it's worth reading both sections regardless of where you end up gardening.

In-Ground Gardening

In-ground gardens are inherited spaces that animals, plants, insects, people, and possibly even another garden inhabited before you came along. The soil holds the story of everything that has been there, whether that includes pollutants from an old factory, compaction from a dug-up concrete patio, or acidic soil from the fallen needles of a nearby spruce tree.

Since most of us can't afford an overnight overhaul, we've got to do the best with what we have and improve conditions slowly. Here's how.

Assessing Your Soil

Soil is everything to a garden. In fact the soil *is* the garden. As gardeners we can't help but fixate on the plants, yet when it comes to the health and vitality of the garden, plants are actually secondary. Soil is a living organism (yep, even the crappy stuff); a mash-up of minerals, fungi, bacteria, air, water, organic matter, and a host of little critters all doing their own thing yet also working together and forming complex relationships with one another. Along with the plants, they carry out a cycle of life and death. The plants derive nutrients from the earth, some of which go back in when the plants die. Without human intervention this cycle goes on and on into infinity. As gardeners we disrupt this equilibrium in an effort to make everything neat and orderly. When we pull plants out at the end of the season, we take away potential nutrition. This is why it is important to make compost (page 46) and add heaps back to the garden every year. Otherwise you will end up taking and taking until nothing remains but a lot of dry and dusty, infertile dirt. Food plants will stay small, grow slowly, become riddled with pests and disease, or become unproductive.

Soil conditions differ vastly from place to place, even within the same yard. To determine what kind of soil you have, follow these steps:

1. Test your pH using an at-home test, available at most garden and hardware stores for just a few bucks.

Most food gardens prefer soil with a pH that is neutral to slightly acidic. If yours is in that golden mean, skip to Step 2. Altering soil pH that swings too far to either side of neutral can be a real pain in the butt. Instead of endlessly adding compost, manure, lime, or other soil amenders, the easiest way to proceed is to build a raised bed on top, kicking all of that inferior stuff to the bottom of the heap. See "Build a No-Till Raised-Bed Veggie Plot" (page 44).

2. Determine the texture of your soil.

Every soil has a distinct texture that you can feel with your hands. Pick up some soil, wet it a little, and run it between your fingers. Does the moistened soil feel gritty and coarse like sand, sticky like clay, silky like silt, or loose and crumbly like loam? If you feel loam, then ding-ding-ding you've won the soil lottery. A mix of sand, silt, clay, and organic matter, loam is not too hard when dry, doesn't stay drenched when wet, and is light with lots of air pockets between the particles allowing plant roots to breathe freely.

If you don't have loamy soil now, you can someday. The trick is to add lots of compost to the garden year after year. For more on composting, see page 46.

Getting the Most from What You've Got

Does your backyard look like Oklahoma in the Dirty Thirties? Have you got a desert or a wetland out back? Is the sunlight being blocked from your balcony by tall trees, high fences, or that new sixteen-story condo? Unless you've got buckets of cash, improving really bad soil conditions can take a couple of seasons—but in the meantime, you can use the chart on the opposite page to start enjoying a little food garden now. Keep in mind that in extreme cases your yields may be lower than expected.

Good Contenders for Poor Conditions

DEPLETED SOIL

The following plants can handle soil with lower nutritional content, making them a good choice for your miniature version of the Dustbowl.

Arugula (*Eruca sativa*)
Blackberry (*Rubus fructicosus*)
Borage (*Borago officinalis*)
Bronze fennel (*Foeniculum vulgare 'Rubrum'*)
Dill (*Anethum graveolens*)
Fennel (*Foeniculum vulgare*)
Lemon balm (*Melissa officinalis*)
Marjoram (*Origanum majorana*)
Mexican sour gherkin (*Melothria scabra*)
Nasturtium (*Tropaeolum majus*)
Oregano (*Origanum* spp.)
Radish (*Raphanus sativus*)
Sage (*Salvia officinalis*)
Thyme (*Thymus* spp.)
West Indian burr gherkin (*Cucumis anguria*)

SOGGY SOIL

Try as you might, this soil will not drain well. Thankfully, the following plants don't mind.

Angelica
Bee balm (*Monarda*)
Lemongrass (*Cymbopogon citratus*)
Mint (*Mentha*)
Rice (*Oryza sativa*)
Watercress (*Nasturtium officinale*)

SHADY SPOTS

I know you are not going to like to hear this, but few edibles will grow in true shade. Fortunately, a small number can tolerate partial shade (4–6 hours of direct sunlight), although the more sun you can provide the better.

Blackberry (*Rubus fructicosus*)
Chervil (*Anthriscus cerefolium*)
Chive (*Allium schoenoprasum*)
Currant, red and black (*Ribes rubrum, Ribes nigrum*)
Garlic chive (*Allium tuberosum*)
Gooseberry (*Ribes uva-crispa*)
Kale (*Brassica oleracea* Acephala Group)
Leafy greens (arugula, lettuce, etc.)
Lemon balm (*Melissa officinalis*)
Mint (*Mentha*)
Pansy and viola (*Viola × wittrockiana*)
Parsley (*Petroselinum crispum*)
Peas (*Pisum sativum*)
Radish (*Raphanus sativus*)
Rhubarb (*Rheum rhabarbarum*)
Runner beans (*Phaseolus coccineus*)
Salad burnet (*Sanguisorba minor*)
Society garlic (*Tulbaghia violacea*)
Sorrel (*Rumex acetosa*)
Spinach (*Spinacia oleracea*)
Swiss chard (*Beta vulgaris* Cicla Group)

HOTTER THAN HADES

These plants can survive short periods of dry soil and won't mind life on your sizzling hot fire escape or balcony.

Amaranth
Anise hyssop (*Agastache foeniculum*)
Borage (*Borago officinalis*)
Dill (*Anethum graveolens*)
Garlic chive (*Allium tuberosum*)
Hot pepper (*Capsicum*)
Jerusalem artichoke (*Helianthus tuberosus*)
Lavender (*Lavendula*)
Marjoram (*Origanum majorana*)
Nodding onion (*Allium cernuum*)
Okra (*Abelmoschus esculentus*)
Oregano (*Origanum* spp.)
Prickly pear cactus (*Opuntia*)
Purslane (*Portulaca oleracea*)
Sage (*Salvia officinalis*)
Thyme (*Thymus* spp.)

Build a No-Till Raised-Bed Veggie Plot

When it comes to growing in the ground, raised beds are the best way to go. They make maximum use of limited garden space and tend to be a lot more productive than your basic in-ground bed. Much of this has to do with the soil. Making a raised bed is the easiest way to achieve premium, loose soil fast, no backbreaking tilling or double digging required. On top of those benefits, raised beds warm up quicker in the spring—the higher the bed, the faster it warms. They're also a little bit elevated off the ground, which means less bending over for you and less chance that the dog will jump on the lettuce.

This method of building a raised bed is both economical and easy work. Instead of turfing sod and purchasing expensive amenders out of a bag, you'll make good soil on top of the grass using compostable materials. It's sort of like building a compost pile that you never turn or move. When it's done, you just plant right into it! Keep in mind that composting takes time—the earlier you start the better. Give the garden a good 4- to 6-month head start if you want to get growing next spring.

Building the Box

Raised beds come in all shapes and sizes and can be constructed from just about anything that will hold itself up or that can be nailed together. Using good-quality, rot-resistant wood turns out a garden bed with longevity, but you can also choose from lots of cheaper options if you don't mind rebuilding or patching up crumbling walls in a year or two. Repurposed wooden futon frames are curbside gold. They are also abundant. Many of us had a futon before stepping up to a "real" couch or bed. Alternatively, assemble broken bits of salvaged concrete, rocks, or cinder blocks as if building a wall.

YOU WILL NEED
- Edging materials (see page 45)
- Rustproof decking screws
- Large landscaping nails
- Plastic sheeting (optional)
- Staple gun and staples (optional)
- Lots of newspaper
- Lots of composting materials (see page 45)
- A cover (see step 5)

1. The best way to begin is by building up the sides of the bed before you start composting the soil. Stick to small beds that are no larger than a few feet wide. A small bed with a center that is accessible from all sides is easier to manage and less likely to get compacted soil from people stepping around in it. Build the edges up directly on top of the sod or soil. Use rustproof decking screws and large landscaping nails to secure wooden planks and timbers together. Use small pieces of wood set inside the corners or old door hinges to secure the sides.

2. Line the sides of the bed with plastic sheeting and staple it in place with a staple gun. This step is optional but can help preserve the life of wooden boards just a little longer or act as a barrier between the soil and foraged materials with dubious origins.

3. Begin to pile up a thick layer of wet newspapers inside the box, about ten sheets thick. Don't skimp out on the paper! This layer is integral to smother the old sod. Wetting the newspaper first prevents it from blowing off and driving you mental.

4. Next, cover the newspaper with any organic materials you can get your hands on. The goal is to overfill the box with a minimum of 10–12" of organic matter. Just about anything that is fit for the compost pile is fair game. The trick here is in how you apply the materials. Sort out everything from the coarsest materials (such as plant clippings) that will take the longest to compost, placing these down first, and working your way up to the finest materials (such as topsoil or finished compost from the bin).

5. Cover everything with some kind of sheeting or blanket. Old carpets and rugs make good covers. So do old, moth-eaten blankets and ill-fitting jeans. Only use blankets and fabrics that are 100 percent natural fiber (cotton, wool, etc.), and be sure to cut out any metal zippers and snaps. Plastic sheeting or black plastic is particularly good for quick-cooking the pile because it will draw on the sun's rays to create heat.

6. Check back with the bed in 4–6 months when you're ready to plant it up. The top layers should be decomposed into crumbly, earthy-smelling soil. If for some reason there is still a lot of partially decomposed matter only a few inches below the surface, replace the covers and let the process continue for a few more weeks. Add more finished compost or topsoil if the soil level is several inches below the top of the bed. Now, get planting!

EDGING MATERIALS

Used timber

Discarded furniture

Futon frames

Cinder blocks

Rocks and boulders

Bricks

Large branches

Broken paving

Rot-resistant wood (cedar and cypress)

Used wooden pallets

COMPOSTING MATERIALS

Newspaper

Twigs and brush

Grass clippings

Leaves

Wood chips

Food scraps

Straw

Compost

Nutshells

Eggshells

Coffee grounds

Topsoil

Yard and garden waste

Aged manure

Making Healthy Soil: Composting in Small Spaces

Composting is an excellent recycling system that replaces the nutrients plants remove from the soil while growing. It is also the cheapest way to improve the texture of your soil, increase drainage, perk up the nutritional content, and bring worms to your garden. All of that for free!

Compost Happens

The hardest thing about composting is finding the space in which to do it. A lot of gardeners learning this skill for the first time tend to get too caught up in the idea of the right way to compost or having the right "system" for it. All it really takes to compost is a trash bin with a bunch of holes punched into the sides and bottom. Even a hole in the ground will do. Fancy systems can be helpful, but they aren't critical. We currently maintain two composters at my community garden. The most successful is a pile loosely held in place with a bunch of broken wooden shipping pallets and wire. It looks terrible but produces piles of quality compost each spring. On the other hand, our ready-made plastic bins have caused an endless amount of misery: the top and bottom pieces constantly fall apart, causing the compost to dry up and become inactive quickly. It got so bad that a few years ago hornets took up residence in the dry brush at the bottom!

If space is not on your side, try managing a small bin on your balcony. Making even a little compost is better than making none at all. Better yet, a worm bin (aka vermicomposter) can be kept underneath the kitchen sink year-round and just happens to make the best all-around fertilizer for container plants.

Increase the fertility of your compost pile by adding slow-release fertilizers like rock phosphate and greensand. Manure should always be composted before going into the garden.

How to Compost

1. Construct a bin using recycled "finds" such as wooden pallets, straw bales, chicken wire, cinder blocks, bricks, stacks of tires, and branches. You can mimic a store-bought bin cheaply by drilling or poking lots of ¼" or larger holes in the sides, bottom, and lid of a plastic tote box, used oil or detergent container, or metal or plastic rubbish bin. Don't skimp on the holes; they're necessary to create good air circulation and reduce stink.

2. You'll also need a lid. Some compost bins work without one, but I find it a whole lot easier to regulate the heat and moisture levels when some sort of blanket or cover insulates the pile and keeps heavy rainfall out. Old throwaway carpets, burlap, tarp, and plastic sheeting will work in a pinch. Keep light covers from blowing away by placing something heavy on top.

3. If possible, set your bin on top of a patch of soil. This will give leaking liquid somewhere to go and allow beneficial insects in. When soil isn't an option, place a tray underneath that can catch the nutrient-rich runoff. That stuff is liquid gold! Set it aside and pour it on your plants when they need a quick hit.

4. Just about anything natural can be composted. But since most of us don't have the space to build a large, more efficient hot compost pile, it's best to stay away from anything that is slow to decay or will draw rodents and other unwanted critters to the pile. The key to maintaining an effective pile is in mixing up textures and providing a balance of nitrogen-rich "greens" (kitchen scraps) and carbon-rich "browns" (dry plant material). Decomposing stops when the mix goes too far in either direction. When filling a new bin or pile, try to layer an equal amount of each, burying the greens beneath the browns. Break up large branches or rotten veggies into smaller pieces before adding them to the pile—the larger the item, the longer it will take to break down.

WHAT GOES IN

Browns (dry, carbon-rich)
Dry grass
Nutshells
Wood
Branches
Dry plant matter
Newspaper and shredded documents
Tissues
Cardboard and toilet rolls
Paper egg cartons and compostable cups
Hay and straw
Used wine corks and matches

Greens (wet, nitrogen-rich)
Veggie and fruit scraps, cores, and peels
Coffee grounds and tea bags
Eggshells
Seaweed and kelp
Horse or cow manure
Used poultry, rabbit, and hamster bedding (herbivores only)
Grass clippings

Keep Out of the Compost
Dog or cat waste
Dairy products and fat
Meat scraps
Anything with oil on it
Laminated cardboard and tetra packs
Magazines
Diseased garden material
Drywall or pressure-treated wood

5. Jump-start a new bin with a store-bought compost activator or beg for some mature compost from a friend with an established bin. Activators get the compost cooking, much in the same way that an accelerant gets an open fire burning. Poultry manure, if you keep chickens in the backyard, is a fantastic activator and a good nutrition-rich addition to the compost pile regardless. Some gardeners swear by the activating power of human urine. Others prefer adding some tea made from comfrey, nettles, or white valerian. Whatever your preference, add a little scoop of activator every time you add new material to a new bin.

6. To keep your pile alive, you're going to need to turn it. Often. Composting is an aerobic process, meaning it thrives on air. Turning the pile moves air in and gets things cooking. Composts that lack air switch to an anaerobic process that is still technically decomposing, although it is a heck of a lot slower and smellier. Aerobic composting should not reek. Turning a large pile can be arm-breaking work, another reason to stay small or go with a no-turning-required worm bin until you've caught composting fever.

7. What you put in your pile and how you composted it determines when it is ready. Large piles produce heat and can be ready to use in as little as a month, but smaller, cold piles that barely register on a thermometer can take a year or more and tend to slow down or stop decomposing completely in freezing temperatures. Finished compost looks dark and crumbly and has an earthy smell. The best stuff usually sinks to the bottom, so check there first if you think your compost is good to go.

NO-BIN COMPOSTING

Rather than yanking dead plants at the end of the season, use this year's crop to build soil on the spot, no work required.

1. Cut back dead, disease-free annuals like tomatoes and beans at the stem, leaving the roots intact to decompose right in the ground.

2. Pile the remaining stems and leaves on top of the soil and add an equal amount of veggie scraps, coffee grounds, grass clippings, and other "greens."

3. Soak the pile with water and cover with sheets of wet burlap or an old blanket.

4. In the spring you should find crumbly rich earth underneath. Discard any remaining large bits in the compost bin or set them aside when you plant the garden, then lay them back on top as mulch.

COMPOSTING PROBLEMS AT A GLANCE

Pests in the Pile: Fly larvae, slugs, centipedes, ants, earwigs, and sow bugs are all commonly seen in compost bins. You've got rotting food in there, so it's only natural that they'd want to get in on the action. They'll even help break things down faster! To keep bugs in check, bury food scraps underneath browns and keep the pile well aerated to increase heat. To keep rodents and mammals out of the bin, bury kitchen scraps well, keep oily food and meat out, or switch to a ready-made bin with a tight lid.

Something Stinks: A stinky, rotten bin smell is often the result of a lack of oxygen. This means either you need to get more air into the pile, or the pile is waterlogged, the result of too much water or too much nitrogen-rich wet stuff. Add more browns to the bin and mix them in well.

Bin Has Been Slimed: Grass clippings and leaves are great additions to the compost, but too much at once can really gum up the works, flattening into a thick, airless mat in the bin. To fix the problem, add more browns to the bin stat and give the pile a good turn.

Nothing Happening: Compost piles that are too dry or heavy on the browns will shut down and stop decomposing. Reignite them by pouring on lots of water, adding in more greens, and giving everything a good stir.

No Backyard Required: Container Farming

Unlike in-ground growing, a container garden is started from scratch, which gives you the advantage of shaping it to suit your desires. This means there's no need to worry about how to deal with hard, compacted soil, because you'll be shipping the soil in. Hate the way you've laid out the garden? No problem, you can move it all on a whim.

Anything from a head of lettuce to a fruit tree can be grown in a container. The trick is in starting things off on a good foot with quality potting soil and in choosing a pot that is ample enough to adequately accommodate the root space of a mature plant. To be fair, the results don't entirely depend on your green thumb: some food plants perform well in containers, while others are known to produce lower yields than in-ground grown plants no matter how big the pot or how determined the gardener. Knowing what works and what doesn't takes some practice (and failures), but to get you off and running, I've provided minimum pot sizes for each plant found in Section 2.

Container-grown plants tend to require more breathing room than in-ground plants. If two plants in a container are crowded, competitions can develop for root space and nutrients, and both plants may end up coming out as the loser. Some plants are space and nutrient hogs requiring their own pot. Plants like cauliflower especially suffer when planted with another of their kind because both plants end up in a battle for the same nutrients. Other kinds with less demanding nutritional needs share space well as long as they are paired with varieties that favor the same light and water conditions but are otherwise unalike. They'll do even better if their nutritional needs are

When combining food plants in pots, pair a single, fruiting plant (tomatoes, peppers) with two or more leafy plants or flowers (lettuce, basil). Or, mix multiple leafing plants together.

divergent. To make the best use of space, plant one demanding, large-rooted plant that grows fruit (such as a tomato) with a couple of easygoing, fast-growing, shallow-rooted plants (such as basil). Everyone's happy.

Container Soil

Although your impulse may be to take soil entirely from the ground and plop it into your container or mix a little in to economize, don't do it. What's good in the garden is disaster in a pot, slowly turning into a hardened clump that will eventually suffocate your plant and rot the roots regardless of how fluffy it was in the ground. Opt for potting soil aka container mix, a soil-like substitute designed to hold moisture well, yet drain freely, all the while remaining light and airy in the pot.

The good news is that this comes from a bag; you won't need to work hard to make it good. The bad news is that commercial mixes vary widely in both quality and price—this is the one place where it really pays to spend a little extra. Some brands are filled with too much peat, perlite, and vermiculite, ingredients that are fantastic for maintaining good air circulation around the roots but lack any soil fertility whatsoever. Peat is a problem ingredient: it can lower the pH of the soil, and the mining that procures it is responsible for destroying wetland ecosystems. Other brands load up on cheap and heavy fillers, creating the compaction you were trying to avoid.

A good potting mix will contain organic matter such as compost, rice hulls, wood chips, and/or worm castings to provide nutrients; perlite, vermiculite, and/or sand to prevent compaction and increase drainage, and coir (a renewable resource and peat substitute derived from coconut husks) to absorb water.

POTTING SOIL AT A GLANCE

Coir: Coconut husk fiber. A renewable resource often used as a peat substitute.

Compost: Highly nutritious organic matter made from rotted plants.

Fertilizer Pellets: Slow-release, synthetic fertilizer often found in nonorganic soil mixes.

Peat: A light and fluffy substrate harvested from wetlands. Highly acidic. Very low nutrition.

Perlite: White, fluffy granules that resemble popcorn. Used to promote good drainage. Good water retention.

Sand: Used as grit to improve drainage and does not retain water well. Be sure to use horticultural-grade sand only.

Vermicompost: Two words: worm poo. A lightweight and nutrient-rich amendment.

Vermiculite: A light and flaky additive derived from mica. Very water absorbent.

Some mixes contain slow-release fertilizers, but if you are going organic look for ingredients such as seaweed, manure, or mushroom compost in place of chemicals.

If your choice at the store is limited, you can always try buying an innocuous base mix and adding in your own nutritional matter and compost. When adding garden compost, use a light hand, adding small amounts at a time. If you'd like to try making your own mix, blend 2 parts coir to 2 parts compost and 1 part grit (sand or perlite).

Choosing Containers

Just about anything that can hold soil can be used as a container. That's good news for your wallet and the environment as you give a second life to something destined for the dump. Recycled pickle buckets, busted watering cans, and empty dresser drawers all make good containers. Even open-weave baskets and fruit crates will work if you line them with a piece of coir liner first. Another way to save cash is by simply switching departments at the store. Garbage bins with a few drainage holes drilled into the bottom are a good substitute for the higher-priced planters found in the garden department.

Terra-cotta: Breathes well but dries out too quickly for moisture-loving plants (lettuce and leafy greens).

Plastic: Holds water well. Opt for recycled pots or biodegradable substitutes made of corn, bamboo, straw, or rice hulls. See page 57 for more on plastic.

Metal: Retains moisture well but absorbs heat like crazy. Poor choice for a fire escape. Utilize broken watering cans and buckets that can no longer hold water.

MATCHING PLANT TO POT

- Envision the plant's mature size (height, width, and root system).
- Opt for large containers that hold water well and require fewer trips to the tap.
- Use small containers for fast-growing crops (lettuce and leafy greens).
- Choose deep containers for root vegetables, tall plants and vines.

Reusing Potting Soil

By the end of the growing season your potting soil will be a shell of its former self, all filler and very little nutrition. Contrary to popular belief, you can reuse container soil. (Keep in mind that any diseases will carry over, so if you've experienced issues, it's best to start fresh.) To reduce problems, you can practice crop rotation (page 35) just as you would with an in-ground garden.

DIY Camouflage: Class up ugly recycled bins and buckets by wrapping them in grass mats, bamboo or wood blinds, or natural fiber rugs, also rescued from the curb. Secure your cover-up with strong twine or wire.

1. Bag up the soil and set aside until spring. Alternatively, leave plastic pots outdoors still filled with soil; empty terra-cotta and ceramics in cold climates and overwinter indoors or they will bust.

2. In the spring, mix 25 percent fresh compost or manure into leftover mix.

3. Add coir, grit, or perlite if the mix seems too dense.

4. Add in supplemental slow-release nutrition. See "Fertilizing" (page 62) for details.

Set It and Forget It (Well, Almost)

A pot that essentially waters itself is a container gardener's fantasy. Although most containers demand a good drink daily if not twice daily, a large self-watering container can provide your plants with a steady drink for days on end.

Self-watering systems are available commercially, but even one box will burn a hole in your pocketbook. This DIY system is built using inexpensive and recycled materials.

How This Works

Building this project requires some experience with measuring and with using power tools and can be a little bit tricky to figure out. In short, this system works by separating a large bin into two sections: one that holds water and one that holds soil. The two sections are divided by a second tote box (the support box) that acts as a large wick, drawing water from the bottom water reservoir chamber up into the top growing chamber.

Maintenance

There is really only one hard-and-fast rule for this system: Do *not* allow the water reservoir chamber to dry out. A dry chamber leads to dry soil; getting things back to normal working order is a bit of a pain. If the soil does dry out completely, fill up the water reservoir chamber and water the soil in the growing chamber until it is thoroughly moist. Once water has been absorbed by the soil right down into the plastic plant pots at the bottom, the system will resume wicking water into the growing chamber.

Fertilize by adding organic dry fertilizers such as kelp meal, bonemeal, or commercially prepared mixes at the time of planting. You can also add some liquid fertilizers such as sea kelp or fish emulsion to the water reservoir chamber when you water.

YOU WILL NEED

- ¼" drill bit
- Drill
- Two square or round plastic plant pots of equal size (minimum 5" deep)
- Two plastic tote boxes or recycling bins of equal size
- Indelible ink marker
- Ruler
- Jigsaw or handsaw
- 2" drill bit
- One large bag well-draining potting soil

Building the Support Box

1. With a ¼" drill bit and drill, make lots of holes—at least twenty per side—in all sides of both of the plastic plant pots. Uniformity is not necessary. The pots are going to function as water-absorbing wicks, so the more holes the merrier.

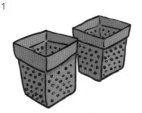

2. Stand one of the plastic plant pots next to one of the plastic tote boxes. Mark the height of the plastic plant pot on the tote box with an indelible marker. Now add another ¼" to the height. Using a ruler, make a straight line all around the tote box marking the height plus a quarter-inch measurement.

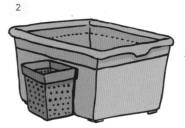

3. Cut along the marked line using a jigsaw or handsaw. Discard the top on recycling day.

4. Flip the tote box over so that the bottom side faces up. This tote box will now be referred to as the support box.

5. The plant pots will be set in the support box and sit in the water reservoir chamber, acting as wicks to draw water up into the top growing chamber. To measure them for this, set one of the plant pots on top of the support box with the bottom side facing down. Position the plant pot within the top left corner of the support box. The position doesn't have to be perfect; 2" or so from the edge will do. Trace around the plastic plant pot with a marker.

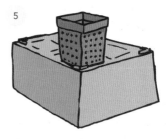

6. Repeat step 5, positioning the second plant pot within the bottom right corner of the support box.

7. Cut each traced shape out of the support box.

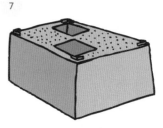

8. With the ¼" drill bit and drill, cover the surface of the support box with lots and lots of holes. The holes don't need to be evenly spaced or measured out—just go nuts with it.

9. Push the two plastic plant pots inside their respective holes in the support box.

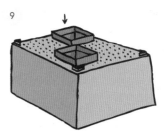

(continued on next page)

(continued from previous page)

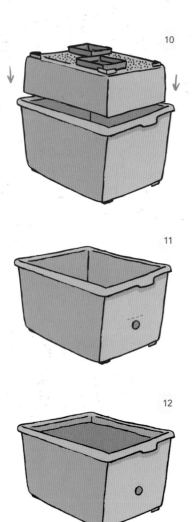

Putting It Together

10. Pick up the entire support box (with all pieces in place) and set it inside the intact tote box. Check the seals between the support box and the outer box. Soil will leak through any cracks into the water reservoir chamber; however, if things don't fit snugly you can always wedge some landscaping fabric into the spaces to seal them up.

11. Using the 2" drill bit and drill, make a hole right through both the outer box and the support box ¼" below the top of the support box. This hole will act as your "fill hole" through which you will fill up the water reservoir chamber. It also acts as a drainage hole, preventing the top growing chamber from flooding.

Filling and Planting the Box

12. Fill the plastic plant pots with premoistened potting soil, packing the soil in firmly. Now, fill the entire growing chamber with the remaining soil to within an inch of the top.

13. Using a hose or watering can, fill the water reservoir chamber through the fill hole. You will not need to moisten the soil in the growing chamber again.

14. You're ready to plant! This system will keep the soil consistently moist but isn't a miracle worker—don't try to overstuff it. Generally speaking, an average-sized tote box or recycling bin should support one large plant accompanied by a couple of small plants (for example, one tomato with three basil plants or one melon and two or three nasturtiums).

Plastic: Not Particularly Fantastic

Although just about anything will work as a container, when it comes to growing food you may want to exercise some caution. Some containers, especially plastics, are made from chemicals that will break down under heat, duress, or time, leaching into the soil and ending up in your food. To select the plastic that is best for growing food, get to know the recycling codes found on the bottom of all plastic containers.

Considered Safer:

1 (polyethylene terephthalate, PETE)
2 (high-density polyethylene, HDPE)
4 (low-density polyethylene, LDPE)
5 (polypropylene, PP)

Avoid:

3 (polyvinyl chloride, PVC)
6 (polystyrene, PS)
7 (polycarbonate, PC)

CHAPTER 5:

Taking Care: Growing Healthy Plants

As a practice, organic gardening means taking our cues from nature and applying what we've learned to meet the needs of our own little patch of Eden. As common sense dictates, the best and biggest harvest comes from plants whose needs have been tended to on time.

Learning to be a good gardener is first and foremost about paying close attention to changes in the garden and then trusting our gut and experience to do what seems right. The best way to gain that experience isn't by kicking butt but by screwing up royally—and repeatedly.

Fortunately many plants are surprisingly resilient—they simply want to grow. Many will survive, thrive, and produce food despite us. The next time you find yourself swearing under your breath about a wilted basil or an unproductive tomato plant, remember that we all mess up. Earning your green thumb isn't just about doing everything right; it's also about allowing yourself to do things wrong.

When to Water

Mistakes in watering probably cause more problems in the garden than anything else. Forgetful gardeners often reprimand themselves for underwatering, but plants can just as easily be killed with the kindness of overwatering. Unfortunately there is no magic formula. All plants are different, and so are the daily conditions in which they live. Plants change through the course of the growing season, requiring different amounts of water at different times. And the climate changes too, of course. Then you've got to factor in long-term change in weather patterns, because no two years are exactly alike. Here's what you need to know about what plants require:

- Young plants, especially recently transplanted plants, are thirstier while getting established.

- Plants that are setting flowers or fruit need a deep drink more often, especially if the fruit is big and watery like a tomato or cucumber.

- Larger plants tend to need more water than smaller ones.

- Container plants need to be watered almost every day, sometimes more in the middle of a heat wave.

- Tightly packed pots are exceptionally thirsty, because less soil is available to retain moisture.

How to Water

Believe it or not, how you water is just as critical as how much you water. Plants that are overwatered either rot or grow lazy, producing shallow roots that put the plants at risk during times of drought. Plants that are watered in small amounts frequently, can sometimes suffer from drought if the moisture doesn't really get to the roots and instead evaporates quickly off the surface. The best way to water is deeply—really giving your plants a good, long soak. When watering by hand is impossible, use drip systems and soaker hoses that release water slowly. It's important to give the water time to penetrate down to the roots of your plant rather than shooting the hose all over the bed and leaves or lightly dusting everything but the soil like a sprinkler. Not only does wetting the leaves waste water, it also creates the perfect breeding ground for fungal diseases.

We all know what happens to underwatered plants; they eventually fizzle out. But it's not just a matter of being burned to a crisp. Plants require water to move nutrients out of the soil and in through their roots. Without enough water, the plant starts to stress out, creating a host of problems such as diseased fruit, tough leaves, or premature seed production. A crisp, dead plant is really only the extreme result of a catastrophe that is in the works bit by bit every time a plant suffers from drought.

WISE WATERING AT A GLANCE

Grow Super Soaker Soil: Add lots of compost to your soil yearly to increase your garden's ability to absorb and retain moisture.

Catch as Much as You Can: Hook up a rain barrel or two to your eaves and harvest free water.

Bigger Is Better: Use larger containers that provide ample root space for each plant so they will stay moist longer.

Water Thoroughly: Really soak the soil when you water to grow deep, healthy roots.

Water the Roots, Not the Leaves: Direct the spray from watering cans and hoses at the soil to keep excess moisture off the leaves and prevent disease.

Marvelous Mulch

Imagine mulch as a cozy, protective blanket spread out on top of the garden. It shelters the soil and subsequently the plants that live in it from extreme conditions such as hot, drying sun; pelting rain; blowing wind; and cold snaps. Mulch locks moisture into the soil and keeps weed seed buried. Even container plants can gain from a little mulch spread on top.

And it gets better still. When compost, straw, leaves, and other organic materials are used as mulch, they decompose on the spot, effortlessly increasing the nutrition and texture of the soil. So let's recap: you'll save time, work, and water, and your soil quality will improve with almost no effort on your part. Really, if you aren't mulching, you should be. Thank you and good night.

Choosing Mulch

Mulch generally comes in two forms, organic and inorganic, with all kinds of variations in between. In the organic department, vegetable gardeners generally prefer straw because it looks good and helps build the soil. When I can get hold of some, I pile it onto my community garden plot in thick layers, at least 6" deep. I've even buried it underneath really bad soil, where it decomposed and fluffed the soil in short order. If you live in the country, straw is an inexhaustible resource that is cheap and easy to come by. Not so for the city gardener. The best time to find it is in the fall when garden centers and supermarkets are selling bundles (at a premium, mind you) as Halloween décor. If you can't find it easily, don't drive yourself crazy. You've got other options.

Regular and readily accessible compost makes a darn good mulch. So does well-rotted manure. I don't recommend store-bought chicken manure for the edible garden unless you know where it comes from. Many chickens are factory farmed in pretty awful conditions, which does not bode well for the kinds of organisms you can unwittingly introduce into your food. Shred some newspaper and pile compost or manure on top of it. Sprinkle grass clippings over closely planted carrots like pixie dust. Pine needles work, although they can lower the pH of the soil if you add too much. Best to use them with acid-loving blueberries and strawberries or add a little to a potato crop—a little acidity prevents a disease called scab. Leaves are another abundant option, but they should be set aside to rot into rich and crumbly leaf mold first. It's easy enough to do.

MULCHING TIPS

Lay mulch thickly around plants, but never cover the crown (where the base of the plant meets the soil). Covering the crown can lead to rot.

Stay away from hay, straw's seedy cousin. You'll end up growing more grass!

Don't forget to mulch container gardens. Stick with light materials that won't compact, such as straw and grass clippings.

Plant fast-growing, shallow-rooted crops as living mulch underneath large plants to shade the soil (see "Underplanting," page 37).

Just rake and bag fallen leaves in plastic shopping bags with a few holes punched into the sides. Set the bags next to the compost bin or some other out-of-the-way spot for about a year.

Weeding

Keeping the edible garden weeded is more than just a matter of aesthetics. Weeds can compete for soil nutrition, sunlight, and root space. Many plants can handle a little competition, but most root vegetables and garlic will turn out undersized without enough personal space to spread into.

In truth, weeds are really nothing more than opportunists; when given a chance they're only too happy to move on in. You can prevent them from entering the fray by keeping empty spaces covered with a thick layer of mulch or popping in a fast-growing radish or lettuce seed as soon as a spot opens up. Planting in groupings rather than rows, or underplanting (page 37) tall plants with short ones, leaves little room for weeds to make their move. Tilling the soil will bring a lot of weeds up to the surface, where they've got a fighting chance to germinate. You can eliminate that problem by side-dressing (page 65) with compost rather than digging it in. Unfortunately, compost can be a culprit too. Only hot compost will kill the seeds that get into the bin whenever you toss in a mature weed. Keep mature plants, especially bindweed or anything that has gone to seed, out of the bin at all cost.

EDIBLE WEEDS
- Chickweed
- Dandelion
- Lamb's-quarters
- Oxalis
- Shepherd's Purse
- Sorrel
- Stinging Nettle

WEEDS THAT ATTRACT BENEFICIAL INSECTS
- Buttercups
- Catnip
- Goldenrod
- Oxeye Daisy
- Queen Anne's Lace

Brew up batches of sea kelp tea and keep it on hand for whenever your plants need a dose of potassium.

Fertilizing

Many people believe fertilizing is, above all, the key to growing good food. The assumption is that the more you feed your plants, the better your harvest will be. Not so! This approach to fertilizing stems mostly from the chemical fertilizer industry, whose goal is to keep you locked into dependency on their product. It is true that when you apply chemical fertilizers to a garden, wham, everything turns green in no time. The problem is, once you've started you can't stop. On the surface that may not sound so terrible, but chemical fertilizers build up in the soil and kill helpful microorganisms. While you are working toward building better soil, the chemicals are busy undoing all of your hard work. This kind of buildup is even worse in containers. Synthetics are loaded with salts, which show up as crusty stuff on the sides of pots. Too much salt can keep plants in a perpetual state of thirst in the same way that consuming a bag of chips can make you desperate for a drink.

Organic gardening depends on building up a healthy, self-sustaining ecosystem in which plants can grow at a stable and steady pace. Good soil that is healthy and loamy has what plants need and dishes it out slowly and steadily, giving them a chance to take in nutrition, adjust, grow, repeat. Dumping a load of liquid fertilizer on a crop, sometimes even the liquid organic kind, can ignite a growth spurt your plants may not be able to handle. It's kind of like doling out a big bag of Halloween candy to a group of ten-year-olds. They'll run themselves ragged and become increasingly cranky before finally crashing. And then there's the next day—one long sugar hangover.

Break It Down

Store-bought bags or bottles of fertilizer come with a set of numbers indicating the kinds and percentages of nutrients contained in the product—similar to the nutritional information on a can of soup. Nitrogen, phosphorus, and potassium (NPK) are most responsible for regulating critical stages of plant development.

Organic fertilizers usually contain smaller amounts of other nutrients and minerals, too. For example, fish emulsion is known for being high in nitrogen, but it also contains smaller quantities of phosphorus, potassium, and even a little sulfur. Sea kelp is much loved for its high potassium content, but is also chockablock full with a vast array of secondary vitamins and minerals.

Necessary Nutrients

Nitrogen (N)

Nitrogen is essential to producing lush and happy leaves, so it's important to make sure that leafy crops like Swiss chard, onions, and lettuce get enough of it. Plants that are low in nitrogen grow stunted, with leaves that look sallow or yellow when they're supposed to be green.

Although nitrogen is the nutrient edible plants tend to use most, it is also really easy to overdo. Plants that get too much nitrogen grow leafy and lush fast, but attention focused on the leaves means that flowers and fruit are often forgotten. Give greedy plants like tomatoes a good amount of nitrogen while they're young but then pull back in time for the plant to start shifting focus to flowers and eventually fruit. Excess nitrogen is also responsible for encouraging plants to grow tall, lanky, and feeble, a condition that will attract aphids to the garden in droves.

Get It: Worm castings and compost are good balanced nutrient sources of nitrogen. Blood meal, fish emulsion, coffee grounds, and manure (in order from highest to lowest) are all high in nitrogen. Grow a crop of peas, beans or other nitrogen-fixing legumes.

Potassium (K)

Potassium produces resilient, vigorous plants that can bounce back after brief periods of stress. This element helps regulate important processes, including photosynthesis and the flow of nutrients through the entire plant.

Potassium deficiency can be hard to spot but is generally responsible for producing thin-skinned, small fruit, or sometimes none at all. Plants appear weak and spindly and are especially prone to disease.

Get It: Greensand is a good slow-release option, rich in trace minerals that can last in the soil for several years. Sea kelp is my favorite source of potassium. Buy it dry and you can add it straight to the soil or brew up a tea to pour on plants or feed foliage.

Phosphorus (P)

Phosphorus is most noted in the edible garden for producing healthy, strong root systems. For this reason you'll want to be sure that your root crops are not lacking in it, especially in their early days. Most sources of phosphorus are slow release. They stay in the soil for long periods of time but are also difficult for the plants to get at. Plants cannot take up phosphorus well if they suffer from drought or the soil pH is too alkaline.

Plants that are deficient in phosphorus tend to grow slowly and have stunted, undersized roots. Root-bound tomato seedlings are notorious for producing leaves with purple undersides. Even corn plants get a little purplish when phosphorus is lacking.

Get It: Bonemeal is a good source of slow-release phosphorus, but because it comes from ground-up slaughterhouse animal bones, it may not be the best choice if you're concerned about the source. If you do use it, apply it yearly. Rock phosphate is good to add when you start a brand-new garden because it releases phosphorus very slowly, over several years. However, it is no good to you if the soil is too alkaline.

Secondary Nutrients

Calcium: Calcium is integral to cellular growth, especially in building cell walls. A deficiency of calcium often shows as blossom-end rot on fruit. See "Blossom-End Rot" (page 72). **Get It:** eggshells, oyster shells, limestone.

Iron: Iron is necessary for chlorophyll production. Iron-deficient plants produce new leaves that are yellow rather than green. **Get It:** foliar feed with sea kelp (page 65).

Magnesium: Magnesium-deficient plants show signs of stunted growth, with older, mature leaves turning yellow and the veins staying dark green. An excess of magnesium can obstruct the plant's ability to take in other nutrients. **Get It:** Epsom salts. See "Epsom Salt Spray" (page 77).

DIY Fertilizers

Coffee Grounds

Coffee grounds are a thrifty source of nitrogen as well as smaller percentages of potassium and phosphorus (in that order). And the best part . . . slugs hate coffee. Sprinkle some around their favorite plants to keep those slimeballs away.

The trouble with coffee is that it is slightly acidic. Adding a sprinkle straight onto the soil around most edible crops is generally okay now and again, but heavy coffee drinkers should save direct application for acid-loving plants like blueberries. Better yet, compost large quantities first and it will be ready to use all over the garden without burning sensitive plants and seedlings.

Crustacean Shells (shrimp, crab, lobster)

Chop up the inedible shells from tonight's dinner and drop them into a 2-foot hole dug in the garden. The shells will compost in a matter of weeks, adding nitrogen, phosphorus, and lime (alkaline) to the soil on site. Mark the spot and dig up the compost in a month or so if you want to spread the goodness around.

Poultry Manure

It smells awful, but chickens make excellent, super-nutrient-rich fertilizer as they soil their bedding. If you're keeping your own chickens, you can't let all of that good stuff go to waste. Put it in the compost bin, bedding and all, for at least 6 months first, because fresh manure is super high in nitrogen and can burn plants.

Comfrey Tea

Comfrey (*Symphytum officinale*) is a doggedly invasive plant that also happens to be chockablock full of phosphorus, potassium, magnesium, and trace minerals and vitamins. You can benefit from its persistence in the garden by turning it into a rich fertilizer tea and feeding all that goodness to the plants that need it. Brew up a batch by mixing 1 part comfrey leaves in a bucket with 2 parts water. Set it in the sun for a day or two to brew, then strain it. Compost the remaining parts and use the liquid as a fertilizer. Dilute it down with water by half or more to use as a foliar spray.

Fish Scraps

Deeply bury uncooked fish heads, guts, and tails in the garden bed where they will break down into the soil, providing lots of nitrogen, trace minerals, and a bit of calcium. Dig holes about 2 feet deep to keep curious critters from nosing around. If you grow in rows, try burying fish parts in between the rows or near nitrogen-loving plants like tomatoes and corn.

Worm Poo Tea

Vermicompost is a great, well-balanced addition to the garden and even better when applied as a liquid foliar feed. If you're keeping a worm bin, there's no reason to buy the store-bought stuff! Steep a couple of tablespoons of worm casting, straight out of the bin, in 4 liters of warm water for about 24 hours and strain it into a spray bottle. If you like, you can even prepackage the castings in paper or muslin filters.

Ways to Fertilize

Just as too much water can drown a plant and cause problems in the garden, too much fertilizer can lead to illness and disease. Take a light-handed approach to fertilizing—most plants are better off a little undernourished than overfertilized. Watch your plants for signs of excess, especially with nitrogen, and cut back if it seems like they are getting too much.

Side-Dressing

Give hungry plants with big appetites an extra boost at critical times when they need it most by adding dry fertilizers or other amenders to the soil alongside each plant. This is generally done once or twice per season, with the first application at planting time and the second after the plants have formed flowers.

For Packaged Fertilizers: Follow package directions for amounts.

For Compost, Vermicompost, and Sea Kelp: Apply a handful or two at most, depending on the size and demands of the plant.

HOW TO:

1. Measuring about a hand's width from the base of the plant, draw a light circle in the soil around plants using your hands, a hoe, or even a kitchen spoon or fork.

2. Sprinkle the fertilizer in evenly and cover it over.

Foliar Feeding

All kinds of fertilizers, including fish emulsion, sea kelp, compost tea, worm poo tea, and comfrey tea, can be sprayed on plant leaves directly to provide a quick boost as a part of a regular fertilizing routine or when plants are down in the dumps. While I've already advised you never to wet the leaves of your plants directly, the fact of the matter is that foliar feeding causes more good than harm—so this is one time when it is okay to break the rule.

To keep things safe for your plants, try to stick to spraying during the coolest part of the day, and be sure to dilute the fertilizer so it won't burn the leaves.

Keep a small bin of red wiggler composting worms in your kitchen and transform kitchen scraps into free fertilizer year-round. They're easy to maintain, odorless, and kind of cute too!

CHAPTER 6:

Garden Under Attack

At the risk of sounding like a broken record, the best way to keep a handle on pests and diseases in the garden is to take a holistic approach and create a healthy environment in which your plants will thrive.

It's not unlike our own bodies: when we're stressed and strained to the limit, we crumble under the weight of a little flu bug like a ton of bricks. And when we're getting our daily vitamins and lots of rest, we're primed and ready to tackle anything that comes our way.

Unhealthy, sick plants are like a beacon for insect pests and disease. Many of us assume that the way to have a pest-free garden and a bountiful harvest is to wipe everything out and create a disease-free and bug-free environment. Unfortunately, the only way to achieve that strange and sterile utopia is at the end of a spray bottle of chemicals. Pesticides and sprays kill or drive off helpful predators, pollinating insects, and countless organisms that do good work in the garden. Interestingly enough, plants need something to resist to help build up their resilience and fight. Killing everything off in the garden makes plants lazy—easy pickings for the inevitable next wave of pests or disease. Try as we might, there will always be more of both.

Creating a balanced ecosystem means that pests and disease still exist, but are unable to grab hold and wreak total havoc in the midst of healthy, resistant, and resilient plants and an army of helpful, hungry predator bugs at the ready. Encouraging these sorts of predators to take up residence in your garden through companion planting is sort of like staging an elaborate battle royal, where the insects do the work and leave you with a little extra time to chill out and enjoy the little microcosm you've created.

Every Garden Hurts . . . Sometimes

To be fair, no garden is perfect or pestilence-free. An occasional infestation of aphids or flea beetles is bound to get through despite your best efforts. Sometimes the weather just isn't on your side, upsetting the balance you worked so hard to maintain. This chapter will introduce you to common problems most food gardeners face and will offer some preventive measures and solutions to which you can turn the next time something hungry finds its way to your tomatoes.

Cucumber beetles may be pretty, but unfortunately ▶
they are not a friend in the garden. Both the
adults and larvae feast on members of the squash
family and can spread viruses between plants.

Know Your Enemy

Identifying the problem early on is half the battle in working out a solution that can save a minor infestation. Even if things are too far gone to rein in an infestation this time, you'll be ready and waiting next time.

The good news for container gardeners is that most of these pests and diseases aren't likely to strike a new garden right away, so you'll have lots of time to get your footing and familiarize yourself with the baddies *before* they find your plants.

Insect Pests

Here are some of the most common garden perpetrators and how to deal.

Aphids

Here's a garden pest that needs no introduction. Aphids are inevitable; every garden, has played host to them at one time or another. You most likely know them as pear-shaped insects with soft, bright green bodies, but they actually come in every color under the sun. Aphids are probably the most persistent of all insect pests, and at times they can be the most destructive, sucking the liquid essence of tender plant parts like some kind of Lilliputian vampire.

How to Deal: Grow marigolds and plants in the onion family to ward them off. Trap them with nasturtiums and cabbage. Attract aphid-eating predators such as lacewings, ladybugs, spiders, and assassin bugs to the garden by growing the plants they love nearby. For more information, see page 75.

Cabbage Butterflies and Cabbage Worms

Cabbage butterflies are easily identifiable as little white butterflies that dance around the garden on sunny summer days from plant to plant. How lovely. Of course, what seems delightful is actually them spreading their evil spawn around your garden! First come the yellow eggs, which eventually hatch into hungry little green caterpillars, chowing down on the leaves of your cabbage family crops.

How to Deal: Protect plants with row covers at planting time and grow celery, hyssop, mint, sage, and thyme to deter the adult moth. Remove the eggs and caterpillars by hand. Plant flowers from the aster family; they'll attract the parasitic wasps that feed on the larvae.

Carrot Flies

Like cabbage worms, carrot fly adults spread their progeny around the garden but the maggots do all the damage, tunneling through developing carrots and other root vegetables underneath the soil.

How to Deal: If you've got a known problem, protect newly seeded beds with row covers. Remove all root veggies at the end of fall, because the flies overwinter in stragglers. Grow susceptible plants alongside known repellents, including onions, rosemary, or sage.

Colorado Potato Beetles

Despite the name, Colorado potato beetles are not restricted to Colorado or potatoes exclusively; they're found throughout North America and have a penchant for stripping the leaves from a variety of edible plants, including tomatoes, peppers, and eggplant, in addition to their namesake. Both Colorado potato beetles and their larvae are easily identified in the garden by their plump and chunky bodies; it must be all those carbs! The beetles have orange heads and black and yellow stripes down their backs; the larvae are orange with little black dots down the sides. You'll find their orange eggs clustered under the leaves of infected plants.

How to Deal: Check diligently under the leaves and remove by hand. A deep layer of straw mulch attracts predacious ground beetles and keeps emerging adults at bay. Alternate potatoes and bush beans and grow garlic, catnip, tansy, and yarrow to repel the beetles and encourage predators.

Cucumber Beetles

Cucumber beetles come in two styles: spotted and striped. Both types prey on cucumber and squash family plants, eating the flowers, leaves, and sometimes the young fruit, stems, and roots. They also like corn, beans, and the occasional pea.

How to Deal: Radishes are said to repel cucumber beetles. The beetles are pretty easy to catch, so controlling by hand is an option. Attract predators such as ladybugs, soldier beetles, and parasitic wasps to the garden. (See "The Popular Crowd" page 37.) Mulch plants with a thick layer of straw to block larvae from emerging from the soil.

▲

While the adult cabbage butterfly may seem innocent, if not downright beautiful, its progeny, the cabbage worm, is a menace to cabbage family crops.

Cutworms

Cutworms are exactly like the name implies: larvae that live in the soil (about an inch deep), cutting through the stems of newly planted seedlings. They're little, but ruthless. Cutworms can kill a new garden overnight, leaving dead plants lying in place as if they had been severed with a knife.

How to Deal: Encourage ground beetles in the garden by mulching with a thick layer of straw. Protect newly planted seedlings with a cutworm collar (page 75).

Flea Beetles

Teeny flea beetles hop around the garden making lots of little holes in the leaves of radishes, eggplant, potatoes, and a few other favorite crops. Infested plants are still edible, just really ugly, as though the plant has been target practice for the world's smallest shotgun.

How to Deal: Protect with row covers after planting. Mustard, nasturtiums, and onions are said to repel flea beetles. These pests prefer to spend their time in the sun; if you can, grow crops in light shade.

Japanese Beetles

Japanese beetles are absolutely stunning, jewel-like insects with iridescent bodies that glimmer in the sun. I'd feel a lot worse about killing them if it weren't for their voracious and indiscriminate appetites. These little critters will eat their way through the garden, leaving defoliated, skeletonized plants in their wake. Nasty!

How to Deal: Rue is said to deter them, but really, where would it be most effective? Japanese beetles love everything. Check plants daily and remove the pests by hand. Attract parasitic wasps with flowers in the aster family. Parasitic nematodes are available commercially.

Mexican Bean Beetles

These spotted nasties resemble ladybugs (which are good bugs) but with rust-colored, plumper bodies. The larvae are almost otherworldly; yellow/orange lumps covered in bizarre

▲

Japanese beetles are a bedazzling scourge that can do serious damage overnight. Adults return to the ground at night, and are best spotted munching on foliage during the day.

spines. Both the adults and larvae can skeletonize a bean plant in a hurry, sometimes causing plants to stop producing or die if the infestation is out of control.

How to Deal: Row covers are the first line of defense for young plants. Plant marigolds and cosmos as repellents or interplant potatoes with bush beans to create confusion. Attract predatory insects with flowering dill and chamomile. Handpick larvae and remove the yellow oval eggs that sit in clusters on the undersides of bean leaves.

Slugs and Snails

Slugs have got to be the worst pest of the bunch. They eat everything in sight and seem to reproduce overnight. Rid the garden of a dozen tonight and there will be twenty more to take their place in the morning. Both slugs and snails like the shade and lots of moisture; they're a source of aggravation and torment during particularly wet years.

How to Deal: Create inviting conditions that will attract their natural predators, including ground beetles, birds, ducks, snakes, toads, centipedes, and lizards. Employ traps and barriers such as containers of beer, copper, and tinfoil collars or a mulch of broken eggshells scattered around young plants.

Squash Vine Borers

These little devils can take down a squash plant fast and furiously. As with many other pests, it's the larvae of adult red and brown moths that cause the real damage. In the spring the larvae hatch and bore into the vines of plants in the squash family, including zucchinis and melons, causing the plants to wilt and die.

How to Deal: Cover newly planted crops with row covers and hand-pollinate. Wrap aluminum foil around the stalk at the base to keep them out. Plant radishes nearby, as they are said to repel them. Regularly check the stems of plants in the squash family, especially near the soil line, for signs of an infestation. If you find any, carefully cut into infested stems and remove the borers.

▲

Check for slugs in the late afternoon when they are most active in the garden and easiest to spot.

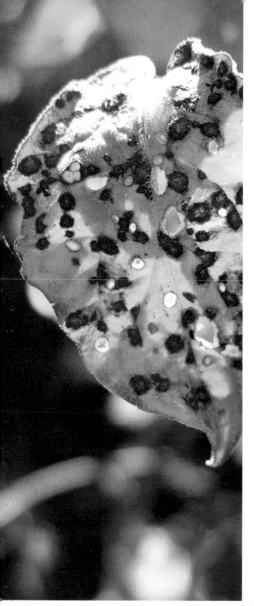

Take precautions against blights and viruses by spraying susceptible plants with diluted milk or compost tea while they are young. Remove any infected plants right away to avoid spread.

Tomato Hornworms

Tomato hornworms are kind of cute when they're not eating their way through your garden. They are recognizable as a large green caterpillar with a distinctive horn on the back end and a taste for the leaves, stems, and fruit of just about any relative of the tomato family they can find.

How to Deal: Basil, borage, and marigolds repel them. Check tomatoes regularly and handpick caterpillars. Attract parasitic wasps.

Diseases

Here are some of the most likely afflictions and the prescriptions to cure them.

Blossom-End Rot

Blossom-end rot appears as a blackened, sunken spot on the bottom of ripening fruit, most commonly tomatoes. Although the problem is technically caused by calcium deficiency, it is often the result of drought rather than a lack of calcium in the soil.

How to Deal: Water your plants deeply, especially containers, taking special care to ensure that the soil doesn't dry out completely. Always grow only one tomato plant per container.

Clubroot

Clubroot is a fungal problem that commonly infects crops in the cabbage family, especially broccoli, cabbage, and cauliflower. The disease is identified by misshapen, deformed roots that lead to wilted and stunted plants.

How to Deal: Clubroot seems to infect only plants grown in acidic soil and can be kept at bay with the addition of lime and some improved soil drainage. Rotate crops and keep brassicas out of previously infected soil.

Cucumber Mosaic Virus (CMV)

Cucumber mosaic virus is often brought into the garden by aphids and transferred to the plants they feed on. The virus can infect tomatoes, peppers, and melons as well as cucumbers. It appears as a yellowish mottling on the leaves, which can also become twisted and deformed.

How to Deal: Encourage aphid predators. CMV can't be stopped once a plant is infected. Remove the plant and practice good crop rotation.

Damping Off

Damping off is a fungal disease that affects young seedlings in their first weeks of life. Too much water, a lack of air circulation, and improper or infected soil welcomes the disease, causing vulnerable plant stems to rot and topple over. Once damping off grabs hold, it's game over.

How to Deal: An ounce of prevention is the best solution here. Grow your seeds in light and airy, sterile seed-starting mix. Don't spray seedlings, but rather water from the bottom by pouring it into the tray and dunk out excess liquid within the hour. Add a little antifungal chamomile tea to your water to prevent damping off before it starts.

Mildew

The most common mildew in the edible garden is powdery mildew, a condition that appears as a gray or white powder on the leaves and flowers of infected plants. This condition thrives in high humidity when there is a lack of airflow around the plant and leaves, but is especially known to target susceptible plants including sage and cucurbits.

How to Deal: Avoid overcrowding plants or spraying leaves. Prune back dense foliage to create better airflow. Spray with Powdery Mildew Brew (page 77).

▲

Prevention is the best defense against powdery mildew, which can be hard to defeat once it has taken hold.

Barriers, Brews, and Backup

Problems are inevitable in even the healthiest gardens. These potions, prophylactics, and partners will lend assistance in averting problems before they start and help get you over the hump when things get out of control.

Fighting Insect Pests

RALLYING THE TROOPS

Luring beneficial insects to your garden is as easy as cultivating the flowers they like to hang around best. To begin, get to know the good guys, including their egg and larval stages, so you'll know whom to remove and whom to leave alone when you're walking through the garden. In many cases the larval stages can be more voracious predators than their adult counterparts. Each helpful insect has a penchant for particular plants; however, it's the flowers that keep them coming, so try to plan so that a few plants are always flowering simultaneously.

THE FIVE-FINGER SYSTEM

It sounds gruesome, but removing insect pests by hand, one or several at a time, is one of the most environmentally friendly and effective methods of control. Snatch caterpillars and beetles straight off the plant and squish them quickly underfoot or plunk them in a bucket of soapy water. Nature is brutal, but we don't have to be malicious about it. Make quick work of it by laying a tarp or newspaper on the soil and giving infested plants a shake.

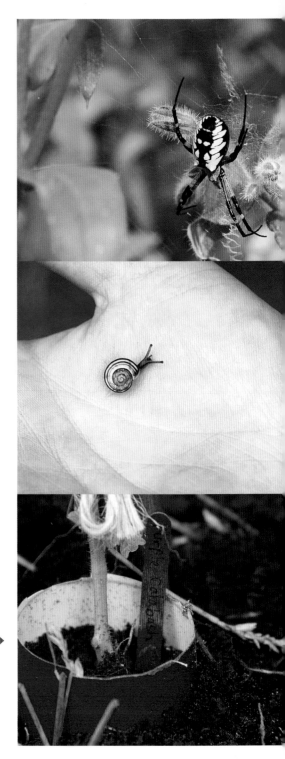

From top: Garden spiders are excellent garden allies and will feast on a wide range of insect pests; the best way to remove pests like snails is by hand, one at a time; even the plastic container your seedling was growing in will work as a makeshift cutworm collar.

CUTWORM COLLAR

Anything that can be fashioned into a tube can be used as a barrier to keep cutworms from taking a bite out of newly planted stems. Toilet rolls work well but can be difficult to slip over well-developed tomato plants. For larger plants, try cutting the top and bottom off water bottles or cans to create a tube.

When planting, be sure to press the tube at least two inches into the soil, because the larvae live in the top inch of the soil. Cardboard tubes will break down on their own, but plastic barriers can be cut off with scissors when the stalk has grown to more than ½" thick.

HOMEMADE ROW COVERS

Drape used open-weave sheer curtains that are out of fashion or headed for the bin over crops that are susceptible to the damage caused by cabbage worms, Mexican bean beetles, and other larvae. The coverage prevents flying adults from laying their eggs on plants in the first place, and you can remove the covers once egg-laying season is over. Stick to light sheers that will still allow sun to get to the plants and moisture if it rains.

SLUG TRAPS

Slimy slugs love moisture in the garden and will flock to a damp, dark spot like flies on manure. A splash of beer in a margarine container is a classic, but you can also trap slugs by luring them to their death with a moist meal. Lay out a cabbage leaf or empty melon rind on the soil surface. The dark underside will be teeming with slugs in no time. Offer the slug-covered meal to the birds or drown the pests in some soapy water.

INSECT PREDATORS

- Assassin Bug
- Big-eyed Bug
- Ground Beetle
- Hoverfly
- Lacewing
- Ladybug
- Parasitoid Wasps
- Praying Mantis
- Spiders
- Yellow Jackets

FLOWERS THAT ATTRACT INSECT PREDATORS

- Aster Family
- Basil
- Calendula
- Catnip
- Cilantro
- Dill
- Goldenrod
- Mint
- Queen Anne's Lace
- Sunflower
- White Valerian
- Yarrow
- Zinnia

Controlling Animal Pests

Whether your garden is on the ground or on top of a building, chances are that you're going to be sharing space with some form of wildlife. I love the starlings that nest in the eaves of my building. Unfortunately, when they clipped and killed my favorite tomato for use in their nest, that love soured temporarily. The following suggestions will help you keep the wild ones off your goods, yet still make them welcome in your safely and humanely run garden. Everyone gets out alive!

- Scare birds off plants by stringing pie tins, broken CDs, and cans together to make obnoxious wind chimes.
- Keep cats off freshly dug soil, even their favorite spot, by covering the area in fresh citrus peels.
- Protect young seedlings from digging squirrels on a nut hunt by surrounding them with a collar made by cutting the top and bottom off plastic bottles found in the recycling bin.
- Craft chicken wire into protective plant cages, lay it across the soil like scratchproof mulch, wrap it around the lower half of pots, or simply cover entire plants to keep persistent raccoons off.
- Leave a handful of used kitty litter in all entrances to a groundhog burrow. The stink can sometimes ward off these otherwise determined critters. You'll have to match their persistence play-for-play if you really want to drive them out.

◄ Wrap chicken wire around the lower half of pots to keep cats and squirrels from digging in the soil.

Combating Disease

POWDERY MILDEW BREW

A mixture of baking soda and water is a classic powdery mildew spray that seems to work if you catch the problem early enough. However, I have found that diluted milk is an even surer bet as both a preventive measure and a fungus fighter once plants become infected. Whenever you've got spoiled or nearly expired leftover milk in the carton, dilute it to a 50:50 ratio and pour the mixture directly on the soil or spray it on the leaves of commonly infected plants. I often dilute the solution with more water early in the season as a preventive but step up the ratio as the humidity and heat rise in the summer. This mix also works wonders to prevent other fungal diseases on tomatoes, zucchinis, and cucumbers. Add a little sea kelp or worm poo tea (page 64) to the mix now and again to do double duty as an all-in-one foliar spray.

EPSOM SALT SPRAY

Cheap and often on hand in the bathroom cupboard, Epsom salts are a great source of magnesium that can help plants when they are struggling to set fruit. Make a mix of 1 teaspoon Epsom salts to 1 quart water. Spray it on pepper, eggplant, and tomato flowers and even some of the leaves when buds first appear on the plant.

DISEASE AND PEST PREVENTION AT A GLANCE

Rotate Crops: Relocating plant families to a new spot in the garden every few years trips up insects and gives the soil a chance to renew (page 35).

Know and Meet Their Needs: Stress caused by overwatering, drought, undersized containers, or other poor cultivation practices can make plants vulnerable to attack (page 72).

Grow Good Soil: Healthy soil leads to healthy, naturally resistant plants (page 46).

Companion Plant: Grow plants in cooperative communities (page 34).

Practice Good Hygiene: Remove diseased plant bits and keep your tools clean, especially after they've been used on sick plants.

Everything in Moderation: There can be too much of a good thing even in gardening. Overfertilizing, especially with nitrogen, can actually cause plants to grow lanky and frail (page 63).

The Plants

CHAPTER 7:

Vegetables

They say that the best things in life don't come easy, an adage that has often applied to my experiences in the vegetable patch. On the one hand, vegetables are typically the most demanding food producers in the edible garden, but in many ways they are the most rewarding. Despite the challenge, and sometimes because of it, I never regret working for the first taste of any homegrown veg.

With few exceptions, vegetables can take longer to put out, so to speak, sometimes requiring months to produce those juicy tomatoes you've been waiting for with anticipation. In the meantime, the plant needs to be kept alive and well cared for. Special attention should be paid to proper nourishment, water, light, and space. Squeezing as many plants into a tight spot as you can always seems like a good idea in the spring when they are small, but you'll pay for it later with smaller yields. One minute those deceptive little tomato seedlings fit in the palm of your hand, the next they're towering above you.

And while we're on the topic of tight spaces, I've included a sidebar entitled "Growing in Pots" for each plant entry that you can use as a guide to navigating the wild and wonderful world of container farming. The good news is that any food crop can be grown in a pot; however, some crops just don't produce abundant yields regardless of the gardener's best efforts, and others are particularly sensitive to the stresses of container life. Use the suitability rating (indicating low-, medium-, and high-yielding crops) as a gauge in planning the most fruitful container garden for your space. Of course, don't let this dictate what's worth growing to you. Productivity is not the only way to assign value in the food garden. Some plants are gorgeous as ornamentals or are a fun challenge regardless of how many soybeans are collected at the end of the season. For this reason I have included favorite varieties that thrive best in pots yet are fabulous in their own right.

When growing plants in containers always keep in mind that they are often happiest, easiest to maintain, and most productive when grown in the largest pots. For the best results, try to avoid growing plants in containers that are shallower than the minimum depth suggested. I've also included additional cultivation tips, tricks, and advice that will give you a leg up on the demands of plants that are particularly finicky.

Diminutive 'Tom Thumb' pea is the perfect ▶
size for a small 8–10" pot. Growing green
peas with red violas makes them pop.

Beans

Beans are wrongly accused of being a boring crop lacking the heady excitement of tomatoes or the flash of Swiss chard. Lies, I tell you! Although it's true that common green beans are a bit dull, plenty of head-turning varieties hang from the vine like colorful, dangling jewelry.

Good Growing

Beans belong to the legume family, plants that supply their own nitrogen through a relationship with *Rhizobia* bacteria that live in the soil. However, because this process takes a while to develop, you will need to supply your plants with nitrogen by adding compost to the soil before planting. Adding compost will also improve soil drainage, which is key to preventing rot, rust, and other fungal diseases. Keep the soil moist but not soggy, especially while the seeds are germinating when the chance for rot is greatest. Water lightly yet steadily early on, increasing the amount once flowers appear. Watch out for leafhoppers and Mexican bean beetles.

Beans grow well alongside most crops, with the exception of members of the onion family.

Wait until the soil has warmed, with air temperatures above 60°F (warmer for soybeans) before planting. Mine usually go in the soil just before the peas make their exit. Soak beans (except soybeans) overnight in your choice of water, compost tea, or seaweed and then dip in *Rhizobia* bacteria inoculant (just like Shake 'n Bake) before sowing. Although *Rhizobia* bacteria occur naturally, adding powdered inoculant to seeds can greatly increase yields. Sow directly into the ground or into toilet paper rolls (see "Toilet Roll Seed-Starting Cells," page 27).

Pick snap beans daily once they get to be ¼" wide, and pick shelling beans when the seeds have swollen inside the pod. Harvest drying beans when the pods go brown and dry out.

GROWING IN POTS

A gorgeous addition to medium- to large-sized buckets and plastic garbage bins, although climbing beans do best in raised beds.

Bush Beans:
Suitability (Yield): High
Minimum Depth: 12"
Varieties: 'Royal Burgundy', 'Contender'
More Tips: Succession plant to keep the harvest coming.

Pole and Runner Beans:
Suitability (Yield): Medium
Minimum Depth: 16"
Varieties: 'San Felipe Pueblo White', 'Rattlesnake Snap'
More Tips: Southwestern (tepary) drying varieties withstand drought best.

Soybeans:
Suitability (Yield): Low
Minimum Depth: 14"
Varieties: 'Tohya', 'Early Hakucho', disease-tolerant 'Jet Black'
More Tips: Sensitive to wet, cold soil. Provide good drainage to prevent rot.

◀ Clockwise from top left: 'Black Jet' soybeans harvested from one 12" pot; a rainbow of colorful beans; shelling beautiful cranberry beans.

Bush and Pole Beans

(*Phaseolus vulgaris*) — Legume Family (Leguminosae)

Bush beans are low-growing plants that produce one crop before giving up the ghost. To grow a continuous harvest, sow new beans every few weeks. Try your hand at varieties with unusual flower and bean colors. 'Royal Burgundy', 'Sequoia', and 'Royalty Purple Pod' all produce purple pods; 'Orca' is a gorgeous drying variety with black-and-white seeds. I especially adore 'Dragon's Tongue', whose flattened pods are adorned with reddish-purple markings.

Although not magical, pole varieties are your classic Jack and the Beanstalk bean, climbing tall and grabbing onto anything in their path on the way up. Training them up a trellis creates height in the garden and allows you to get A LOT of food out of a small space. No exaggeration. They will produce for weeks on end. Beautify your space and your plate with 'Gold of Baucau', a flat, brightly golden bean; 'Rattlesnake Pole', whose green pods are covered with purple streaks; or 'Trionfo Violetto', a yummy variety with purple flowers that lead to purple beans. Better yet, try 'Cherokee Trail of Tears', an aptly named reddish/brown pod with black dried beans that sustained the Cherokee people through the tragic forced relocation to Oklahoma in 1838.

Runner Beans

(*Phaseolus coccineus*) — Legume Family (Leguminosae)

Runner beans are very ornamental old-fashioned climbing beans known for their large pods and beautiful flowers that attract bees, butterflies, and hummingbirds to the garden. Grow them in extra-large pots or in the ground just as you would pole beans. Try the classically stunning 'Scarlet Runner' or equally beautiful 'Painted Lady', which produces bicolor red-and-white blooms and pretty speckled dried beans.

Soybeans

(*Glycine max*) — Legume Family (Leguminosae)

Soybeans (aka edamame) are a Japanese delicacy that are fun to eat come harvest time served straight out of the pod, freshly boiled and salted. You'll be surprised by 'Agate', a beautiful heirloom with a reddish-brown bean.

Soybeans can be grown just like regular bush beans but are particularly fussy about soil warmth and moisture, especially during germination. Wait until temperatures reach 70°F and plant the beans about 1–2" deep and 2" apart, straight out of the package without any presoaking. It's okay to presoak other beans, but soybeans will rot without fail.

For the most delicious snap beans you will ever eat, roast young pods in the oven with a sprinkle of olive oil and salt. Yum.

Brassicas

Brassicas, aka the cabbage family, are a famously maligned group, disliked by small children and former U.S. presidents alike. Predictably, our prejudices are the result of a lifetime of suffering through meals of the same boring handful of factory-farmed mainstays. Once you've grown an orange cauliflower or tasted purple broccoli, you may start to wonder what else politicians are wrong about!

Good Growing

Known also as "cole crops" or mustard family plants, brassicas share similar needs and grow well side by side in the garden. They thrive best in rich soil and prefer plenty of sun but will happily tolerate light shade. Don't skimp on the nitrogen, as they need it to grow big, healthy leaves. Work lots of compost into the soil in the early spring and add a scoop directly to the hole at planting time.

Brassicas are cool-weather plants; however, they tend to be sensitive to lower temperatures at planting time and during the flowering stage. They are also quick to bolt in high heat. The trick is getting them in the ground early, just not *too* early. Plant alongside friends like calendula, carrot, cucumber, dill, lettuce, mint, plants in the onion family, and sage. Brassicas do not appreciate the company of pole beans or strawberries.

Broccoli and cauliflower are cherished for the heads, but few people know that the leaves and stems are also delicious—nothing wasted! The heads themselves are actually very large clusters of flower buds and should be harvested while the buds are still firm, before they begin to bloom. Cutting off the first big head signals new smaller heads called *side shoots* to pop up. The faster you harvest these succulent sprouts, the more you'll get, so get busy!

The cabbage family's greatest foe is the cabbage butterfly, but the plants are also known to suffer under aphids, slugs, flea beetles, and cabbage root fly. Covering your plants with a row cover just after planting is your best defense. See page 75 for more. Stress created by consistently low temperatures, drought, too much heat, or a lack of nitrogen can cause broccoli and cauliflower to "button," putting out sad, undersized heads. Clubroot (page 72), caused by acidic soil, is also common.

GROWING IN POTS

Grow one plant per pot, and two to three in wide tote boxes.

Broccoli:
Suitability (Yield): Low
Minimum Depth: 12–16"
Varieties: Small hybrids perform best. Try 'Small Miracle'.

Cabbage:
Suitability (Yield): Medium
Minimum Depth: 12"
Varieties: 'Early Jersey Wakefield', 'Cairo', 'Gonzales'
More Tips: Grow compact, early, and main-season varieties that can be harvested early.

Cauliflower:
Suitability (Yield): Low
Minimum Depth: 12–16"
Varieties: 'Idol', 'Cheddar'

Kale:
Suitability (Yield): High
Minimum Depth: 10–12"
Varieties: All

Broccoli

(*Brassica oleracea* Italica Group) — Cabbage Family (Cruciferae)

Love it or leave it, broccoli does the body good and is chock-full of vitamins, calcium, and antioxidants.

Broccoli can handle a light frost, growing best when the temperature is still on the cool side of the thermometer (around 65°F). For something different beyond the standard green 'Calabrese', try 'Romanesco', a well-loved, although slightly finicky variety that develops a wild-looking lime-green fractal head.

Gardeners living in regions with warm and temperate winters should take a stab at growing sprouting broccoli, a fantastically ornamental plant that is hardy to just below 10°F. Each plant can grow 2' tall and produces lots of small, succulent white or purple sprouts bypassing a large main head. Set transplants out in the late summer and overwinter them, and you'll be rewarded with a generous crop come early spring.

Sow broccoli seeds indoors 6 to 8 weeks before the last spring frost. Transplant seedlings outside when they are 4 to 5 weeks old, spacing them about 15" apart. Start a fall crop 12 weeks before the first frost date in your region.

Cut stems about 6" below the heads when they are full but still tight. Act fast before the yellow flower buds start to open and keep removing any side shoots quickly to get the most from each plant.

Cabbage

(*Brassica oleracea* Capitata Group) — Cabbage Family (Cruciferae)

Cabbage is a good producer, packing a lot of food into a tight package. Plants run the gamut from enormous, leafy globes to smaller baseballs, so consider your space when choosing a variety. If cabbage worm is an unbeatable problem in your garden, try a red variety like 'Mammoth Red Rock'—reds are less susceptible to cabbage worm damage. 'January King' is a solid choice in temperate climates and will survive through the winter as a late crop.

Start cabbage seeds indoors 6 to 8 weeks before the last frost date. Transplant outdoors 3 to 4 weeks before the last frost. Allow a good 10" to 12" between transplants, adding a bit more for behemoth spheres. No need to worry about the young 'uns; they can take a light freeze. Start a fall crop 12 weeks before the first frost date.

Off with their heads or just pull up the whole plant while the leaves are still tightly packed. Harvest stragglers before the first hard frost.

Cauliflower

(*Brassica oleracea* Botrytis Group) — Cabbage Family (Cruciferae)

Sun exposure causes the flower buds (aka curds) of most white cauliflower varieties to naturally discolor and turn yellowish. Yellow heads are edible, but if brighter and whiter is your preference, bind the center leaves with an elastic band or string as the heads begin to form. Save the effort and grow a "self-blanching" variety like 'Snowball', whose leaves fold over on their own. Better yet, go for colorful varieties like 'Violetta Italia' and 'Purple of Sicily'.

More temperamental than other brassicas, cauliflower needs slightly warmer soil to get going in the spring, yet bolts quickly if the thermometer soars too high during the flowering stage. To avoid problems, sow seeds indoors about 4 to 6 weeks before the last frost date and transplant when the temperature is about 60 to 65°F. For a fall crop, direct-sow outdoors in midsummer, a good 18 weeks before the first frost. Space plants about 14" apart.

Harvest when the heads are still compact but are no longer rock solid to the touch. Unlike broccoli, cauliflower does not produce new shoots—once the head is off, it's done.

Kale

(*Brassica oleracea* Acephala Group) — Cabbage Family (Cruciferae)

In the cold north, a frilly-leafed kale on the front stoop is as sure a sign of fall as piles of colorful leaves or smashed pumpkins. The foliage is exceptionally ornamental yet about as hardy as they come, able to survive a snowy winter and provide edible greenery when everything else has long since been done in. Choose from an assortment of colorful, shapely varieties like the bumpy, blue-green 'Lacinato' (aka dinosaur kale) or 'Redbor', whose frilly, deep purple leaves are simply stunning alongside 'Tricolor' sage or ruby 'Red' shiso.

Sow seeds indoors 6 weeks before the last frost or direct-sow outdoors 4 weeks before the last frost. Grow plants closely for young leaves or provide a 15" gap if you want to grow them to maturity.

Harvest kale at any size starting with month-old baby leaves for salads, or let kale grow all the way to maturity. It tastes best plucked just after a light frost.

From top: Harvest the smaller sideshoots from broccoli plants to increase your bounty; bold 'Violetta Italia' cauliflower adds a burst of color to a drab spot; 'Lacinato' kale boasts attractive blue/grey foliage.

Cucumbers

(*Cucumis sativus*) — Cucurbit Family (Cucurbitaceae)

Nothing beats a crisp and crunchy cucumber harvested fresh off the vine, sliced, and sprinkled with salt. Because unusual varieties come in all shapes, sizes, and colors, there's really no reason to restrict yourself to the typical green, elongated version. There are even miniature plants for the truly space-deprived gardener.

Good Growing

Cucumbers prefer bright, warm locations but will tolerate a spot that receives a minimum of 4 to 6 hours of direct sun per day. A sheltered, wind-safe spot backed by a heat-absorbing wall is ideal. Cucumbers are finicky when it comes to water, but once you've got it down the rest is a breeze. They are a juicy vegetable requiring a lot of water to keep them from drying out and turning bitter, undersized, and tough on the vine. You'll find that your plants will require even more water as they mature and produce fruit.

Grow classic varieties such as 'Japanese Climbing', 'A & C Pickling', and the ever-popular 'Marketmore' for reliably high yields. Make cute and compact gourmet pickles from 'Cornichon de Bourbonne', 'Parisian Pickling', and 'White Wonder'. For something truly different, there are yellow ('Boothby's Blonde'), white ('Miniature White'), and orange ('Chinese Yellow') varieties.

Cucumber plants are notoriously susceptible to powdery mildew (page 73) brought on by a lack of air circulation or drought stress—so don't let the soil dry out! Insect pests like aphids and cucumber beetles are a nuisance that can also infect plants with the unbeatable disease cucumber mosaic virus. Crop rotation helps confuse these pests. Plant cucumbers with bush beans, dill, lettuce, nasturtium, peas, and radishes, but keep potatoes at a distance.

GROWING IN POTS

Keep the soil consistently moist for best harvest and juiciest cukes.

Dwarf Cucumber:
Suitability (Yield): Medium
Minimum Depth: 8"
Varieties: 'Patio Pik', 'Bush Pickle', 'Patio Pickles', 'Salad Bush'
More Tips: Not the tastiest but great in very tight spots.

Cucumber (Vines):
Suitability (Yield): Medium
Minimum Depth: 15"
Varieties: 'Lemon', 'Bushy', 'Miniature White'
More Tips: Train up a trellis or stake to save space and support vines off the ground.

Refreshing Cold Cucumber, Mint, and Yogurt Soup

I was first introduced to the concept of cold soups during a high school stint working in a sweaty kitchen. The idea of a no-cook soup sounded like crazy talk until then.

Cucumbers are a classic cold soup staple, often flavored with dill or mint, both of which are abundant in the garden during peak cucumber season. And while I have tried this a hundred and fifty ways to Sunday, I prefer this fresh and simple, quick-make recipe best.

1. Combine the cucumbers, mint, yogurt, coriander, and lemon juice, if using, and 1 cup water in the bowl of a food processor or blender. Purée until smooth.

2. Chill before serving.

3. Season with salt to taste, ladle into bowls, and garnish each bowl with borage flowers, if desired.

Serves 4

- 1 pound cucumbers, peeled and chopped (approximately 8 small)
- 4 tablespoons chopped fresh mint
- 1½ cups plain yogurt
- ½ teaspoon ground coriander seed
- 1 tablespoon lemon juice, optional
- Salt
- ½ cup borage flowers, optional

Sowing and Planting

Sow cucumber seeds indoors in pots approximately 2–4 weeks before the last frost date and ½–1" deep. Transplant the seedlings outdoors well after the last frost, when the temperature is at least 75°F. When transplanting, dig in lots of aged manure or compost and take care not to disturb the roots too much. Choose a mild, gray day to set them out.

Harvesting

Expect to start harvesting in midsummer. Frequent harvesting will keep fruit production going until the first frost. Cut or twist off even the big varieties when they are no larger than 6".

Top down: Grow a single 'Miniature White' cucumber plant in a 15" container; 'Mexican Sour Gherkin' produces slightly sour fruit that look like tiny doll-sized watermelons (adventurous growers will get a kick out of gherkins, the garden cucumber's tinier cousin); Dwarf 'Salad Bush' is suited to a small pot.

Eggplants

(Solanum melongena) — Nightshade/Tomato Family (Solanaceae)

Eggplant is a rather exotic vegetable available in freakish, alien-like forms that totally defy the classic big purple egg made famous in Italian cuisine. In the garden even the plant itself is attractive, with striking, velvety soft leaves and pretty flowers that pair well with purple and red plants.

Good Growing

Hailing from hot and light-filled climates, eggplant requires a sunny spot in the garden with rich soil that drains well. It is a highly temperature-sensitive plant that shrinks from the cold and stops producing fruit if the heat climbs too high. Plants are happiest between 70°F and 85°F—anything lower is bad news. Too much of a good thing is equally damaging, so give them some shelter during particularly nasty heat waves. Just about every pest in the book—Colorado potato beetles, flea beetles, aphids, and everything in between—loves eggplant. They are also susceptible to many tomato diseases. Keep plants happy with lots of nitrogen and a little bit of phosphorus and potassium now and again. Stake tall varieties with long and heavy fruit to keep plants standing and fruit off the ground.

Eggplant doesn't mind sharing space with basil, beans, peas, and peppers but should be kept away from fennel.

Sowing and Planting

Sow indoors well before the last frost, at least 6–9 weeks. Eggplant young hate being transplanted. Start seeds in larger 4" pots and transplant outdoors a good 15" apart at least 3 weeks after the last frost, when the nighttime air is consistently warm (70°F). Use a cutworm collar (page 75) to protect young roots.

Harvesting

Snip new blossoms about a month before the first frost to focus the plant's energy on ripening remaining fruit. Overripe eggplant is dull-looking, bitter, and flabby, so pick eggplant while the skin still has that new-car sheen.

GROWING IN POTS

An advantage for cold-climate gardeners who can't provide the perfect growing conditions in the ground.

Eggplant:
Suitability (Yield): High
Minimum Depth: 10"
Varieties: 'Little Prince', 'Little Fingers', 'Lao Purple Stripe', 'Striped Toga'
More Tips: Small fruit are more drought resistant.

Lettuce and Leafy Greens

Delicious and diverse, salad greens are a supremely easy crop to grow and can be tucked into the smallest spaces, making fresh and inviting homegrown salads possible for just about anyone with a bright window and some soil.

Good Growing

Leafy greens contain a lot of water, so it only stands to reason that they need a steady supply of *agua* to keep them tender and tasty. Problems are most often caused by heat; greens hate it. They are by-and-large cool-weather crops that like full sun but will dash to the seed-making stage of life, or bolt, if the heat is too intense and punishing.

In the summer, grow quick-harvest "cut-and-come-again" greens (aka mesclun mix) that are meant to be harvested young before the plants have a chance to bolt. Cover larger plants with shade cloth or grow them in the shade of taller, leafy crops, a mutually beneficial arrangement for everyone involved.

Start seeds directly outdoors in the early spring as soon as the soil can be worked. Don't bother buying transplants; direct-sown seeds grow into healthier, longer-lasting plants.

Continue to sow small crops every few weeks throughout the spring and later in the late summer once the temperature has cooled off some. Many greens seeds will not germinate in high heat. To sow, spread seeds on the soil surface and cover lightly with a thin layer of soil. Thin the plants out to about 6–8" apart when growing to maturity.

Harvest greens at any size that catches your fancy. Microgreens and baby greens are ready to eat in less than a month, or you can wait until full heads develop and reach maturity. As long as you leave a stub of plant above the soil, plants can regenerate a new head. Creepy, but in a good way. You can repeat this process two or three times with the same plant before the leaves start to taste like a rubber ball. Pull the whole thing up and start again with fresh seeds.

Clockwise from top left: Grow your salad ▶ fixings together in a bucket, as shown here with 'Mascara' leaf lettuce and dill; compact mâche is suited to life in a recycled fruit crate; make an impact by pairing chartreuse and red leaf lettuce; start spinach in early spring for a cool-weather harvest.

WHAT'S THE DIFFERENCE?

Butterhead: A type of head lettuce that forms loose rosettes of tender, "buttery" leaves.

Crisphead: Better known as 'Iceberg' lettuce, a popular crisphead variety that mistakenly represents the whole group. As predicted, these are crisp and crunchy lettuces with juicy, tightly packed leaves that make the plant bolt resistant and heat tolerant.

Leaf Lettuce: Tender and delicate leaves develop into a very loose head that can be plucked as needed. 'Red Sails' and 'Black-Seeded Simpson' are bolt-resistant varieties.

Romaine: Also known as 'Cos', this is the popular Caesar salad lettuce that forms tall, elongated heads of crisp and crunchy leaves. They're another good bolt-resistant choice for hotter climates.

Winter: These cold-hardy varieties keep going straight through the winter in temperate climates but need the protection of a cold frame in colder zones.

Arugula

(Eruca sativa) — Cabbage Family (Cruciferae)

If you've only got space for one leafy green I recommend arugula. It's exceptionally cold-hardy and tough, providing tender, spicy leaves from very early spring into late fall and beyond, depending on your climate. The summer heat turns the leaves a little too peppery, but I just steam those slightly and use them as a pizza topping or in pesto. Pull out plants that bolt and start anew, or keep them going for the flowers, which are also delicious.

Arugula is really easy to grow and will self-seed if you let it. Only a few varieties of arugula exist, and all bear that distinctive peppery bite. 'Rocket' is the most popular, with a reputation for growing fast and furiously.

Lettuce

(Lactuca sativa) — Aster/Composite Family (Asteraceae)

Lettuce is anything but boring. And with gazillions of varieties available, there is no reason to grow just one. I am slowly making my way through all of them, but I'm particularly partial to plants with the richest reds like 'Mascara', 'Lolla Rossa', 'Galactic Red', 'Cimmaron', and 'Selway'. They provide striking, eye-catching contrast when paired with chartreuse-leaved beauties such as 'Lingue de Canario', 'Bunte Forellenschluss', and 'Black-Seeded Simpson'. All that and lunch for pennies a plant!

Eventually even the toughest varieties will succumb to the heat of summer and bolt, rising into interesting Dr. Seuss–like towers that sprout delicate flower tentacles from the center. I always keep a few for their aesthetic appeal, but it's not all vanity; they'll ultimately make a heck of a lot of seeds, ensuring next year's crop and then some.

Mâche

(Valeriane lla locusta) — Valerian Family (Valerianaceae)

I used to think mâche was overrated and overpriced until I had it done up right, the tender rosettes salted and paired with a sharp cheese and slices of ripe plum.

Mâche, also known as 'Lamb's Lettuce' and 'Corn Salad', may be billed as a pretentious food, yet it can be grown as cheaply and easily as any other green. The plant is a little bit fussier and slower-growing than other greens, but it is also the hardiest (to 0°F), making it a rare winter crop that can be picked even when frozen.

Unlike most greens, mâche really demands cool weather to get germinating. Skip the spring and summer and direct-sow the seed in late summer for an autumn and early-winter harvest.

Chop off whole rosettes right at the soil line, leaving the delicate roots in the ground. Mâche will not produce another plant, but it will put some nutrients back into the soil.

Mustard Greens

(*Brassica juncea*) — Cabbage Family (Cruciferae)

Mustard greens are primarily known for packing a spicy kick, although there are mild types like tatsoi with flavors that are subtle yet much more distinctive than lettuce. Mizuna is also quite mild, with a light tang that makes it a good overall salad green. 'Giant Red Mustard' and 'Osaka Purple' are two of the flashiest of the group, growing into large, bold, and beautiful plants with shimmery, almost iridescent leaves that eventually sprout tall stalks of yellow flowers. Both the leaves and the flowers are HOT like a radish.

Mustard greens are a somewhat cold-tolerant group that tend to attract pests like leafminers and sometimes aphids if neglected.

Many mustard greens taste best as sprouts, an easy year-round crop for the windowsill (see "No-Space Grub," page 14). Start cutting off leaves at just about any size, remembering that the larger they grow, the tougher and spicier they become.

Spinach

(*Spinacia oleracea*) — Beet Family (Chenopodiaceae)

No food garden is complete without this versatile and healthy "superfood," and nor should it be because spinach is a near no-brainer that can be grown just about anywhere. In the spring, grow a slow-bolting variety such as 'American Spinach' or 'Bloomsdale' that will keep trucking into the early summer heat. In late summer, plant 'Giant of Winter', a variety that can't stand the heat but will survive the winter under a blanket of straw mulch.

Pull out the entire plant in midsummer as soon as flower buds appear and replace it with a heat-loving spinach substitute such as 'New Zealand' (*Tetragonia tetragonioides*) or 'Red Malabar' (*Basella rubra*).

OTHER GREENS TO TRY

Amaranth

Claytonia aka miner's lettuce (*Montia perfoliata*)

Cress (*Lepidium sativum*)

Egyptian spinach aka Molokheiya (*Corchorus olitorius*)

Endive (*Cichorium endivia*)

Lamb's-quarter (*Chenopodium album*

Minutina 'Erba Stella' (*Plantago coronopus*)

Purslane (*Portulaca oleracea*)

Quinoa (*Chenopodium quinoa*)

Radicchio (*Cichorium intybus*)

Red orache (*Atriplex hortensis*)

Salad burnet (*Sanguisorba minor*)

Shungiku (*Chrysanthemum coronarium*)

Sorrel (*Rumex acetosa*)

Strawberry spinach (*Chenopodium capitatum*)

Turn around bolting to your favor: Grow stem lettuce, 'Cracoviensis', a variety that produces crunchy and sweet stalks that are better than celery.

Living Mulch: Grow more food and shade the soil by planting quick-growing lettuce crops underneath tall leafy plants like tomatoes, okra, and eggplant.

Onion Family

Even if onions, garlic, chives, and other members of the onion family are not your cup of tea in the kitchen, they are worth growing in the garden as a devoted bedfellow for most food crops. Alliums are naturally odiferous plants, a handy trait that confuses insect pests and deters them from having lunch in your garden.

Good Growing

Alliums are extremely tough plants. I've found onions and chives growing all on their own in the remnants of long-abandoned gardens and rising straight out of the lawn where bulbs were accidentally dropped in transit to the compost heap. Almost any garden space or pot can accommodate them, as they will happily tolerate less-than-ideal conditions, including partial shade to poor soil. Just be sure to give them their space and keep out the weeds—plants in the onion family will turn out small and miserable in crowded quarters.

Water deeply when the soil starts to dry to ensure a good crop. Uneven watering, especially when containers dry out, can cause the bulbs to split. Keep them watered and they will do well in containers, especially chives. They're one of the first crops to pop straight up as soon as the snow melts, stronger than ever.

Chives and Garlic Chives

(*Allium schoenoprasum*) and (*Allium tuberosum*) — Allium Family (Liliaceae)

Although considered herbs, chives and garlic chives are actually the smallest members of the onion family. Although the focus is on the leafy parts and sometimes the flowers, the little bulbs are also worth harvesting a few years in, once the crop size inevitably starts to get out of hand. Even the seeds are useful and taste great when sprouted on a windowsill and served on salads or sandwiches (see "No-Space Grub," page 14).

GROWING IN POTS

To prevent rot, keep pots consistently watered but not soggy.

Chives:
Suitability (Yield): High
Minimum Depth: 4–6"
Varieties: All
More Tips: Very cold-hardy, even in a container. Grow on a windowsill and snip off grassy greens.

Garlic:
Suitability (Yield): Medium
Minimum Depth: 8–12"
Varieties: 'Persian Star', 'Siberian'
More Tips: Require extra-large bins to produce bulbs but can be planted in the early spring to turn out green garlic midway through summer.

Leeks:
Suitability (Yield): Medium
Minimum Depth: 10"
Varieties: 'Mammoth Pot Leek', 'Bandit'
More Tips: Mound soil up around plants as they grow.

Onions and Shallots:
Suitability (Yield): High
Minimum Depth: 6–8"
Varieties: 'Purplette' onion, 'French Shallot'
Additional: Start large-bulb varieties from seed and pull when tops are 6" tall for tender scallions.

Onions (Bunching):
Suitability (Yield): High
Minimum Depth: 6"
Varieties: 'Crimson Forest', 'White Lisbon'

Clockwise from top left: Red onion sets ready for spring planting; hardy 'Egyptian Walking Onions' will self-perpetuate into perpetuity; mild-tasting garlic "scapes" are a favorite early summer delicacy; these leeks are putting out buds that will soon bloom into a showy globular flower.

Unlike most alliums, chives are grown as perennials, popping up year after year from the tiny bulbs that stay in the ground indefinitely. They will also self-seed like mad, so cut off the flowers (and eat them) if you don't want a garden full. There's not a lot of variation to choose from; however, for something offbeat try 'Garlic Chive Mauve'. It sprouts pale lavender flowers in the early fall instead of the usual white.

Harvest all chives throughout the growing season by clipping fresh leaves straight off the top with scissors, just like mowing blades of grass.

Garlic

(Allium sativum) — Allium Family (Liliaceae)

Garlic comes in two main types. Soft necks are a good choice in southern climates, but they are not hardy enough to withstand cold winters up north. Stiff necks, on the other hand, are super hardy and keep well for ages.

To grow bulbs, plant garlic in the early to late fall, about a month or two before the ground freezes. To begin, gently tease apart the larger bulb into individual cloves, saving the largest and healthiest for planting. Eat the rest for dinner. Next, make lots of 2–3" holes in your chosen spot of earth with a stick or planting tool, spacing them about 4" apart. Pop one clove into each hole with the pointy end sticking up and cover everything over with fresh soil and a layer of straw mulch.

In the very early spring, scratch a little extra compost into the soil and water well, keeping the soil evenly moist. Too little water and your garlic will grow undersized. Too much and you risk rot.

Alien-like flower buds called *scapes* should show up around midsummer. Cut them off low on the stem to keep energy focused on making good, healthy bulbs. Scapes are considered a delicacy—you'll have your own supply!

Dig up entire bulbs in the late summer or early fall just after the leaves begin to turn brown and droop. Hang them to dry (aka cure) in a dry spot for a couple of weeks and save the largest cloves for replanting next year's crop.

Leeks

(Allium ampeloprasum Porrum Group) — Allium Family (Liliaceae)

Of the alliums, leeks tend to be the most demanding about nitrogen, preferring to be grown all on their lonesome where they can hog it all for themselves. Buy transplants if you're pressed for space and time. If you do go the seed-starting route, sow indoors 10–12 weeks before the last frost. Plant transplants a week after the last frost, spacing them approximately 4" apart. For the softest, best leeks, grow in trenches or plant deeply (about 4") and hill up the sides, adding soil mixed with a touch of compost throughout the growing season.

In warmer climates, start harvesting small leeks in midsummer and straight through into the next spring. The rest of us need to dig them all up before a hard frost hits.

Onions and Shallots

(Allium cepa) — Allium Family (Liliaceae)

Onions are less picky about soil than leeks and garlic; you'll be able to knock out something edible, albeit on the small side, in less-than-ideal conditions. Still, everyone will be happier if you go the extra mile by adding compost to the soil in early spring. Onions come in all shapes, sizes, and colors, with some varieties that are hardier than others. To keep the harvest coming, even in cold climates, I favor 'Egyptian Walking

Onions', named for their peculiar growth habit. This particularly ornamental type reproduces from bulbs that grow out of the top of the plant. The added weight causes them to droop and take root in the soil, spreading around the garden as if "walking" on their own. You can eat the topsets or allow them to root themselves for the earliest spring crop.

Options abound when it comes to getting onions growing. The slowest method is to start seeds indoors about 2 months before the last frost. Grow onion seeds in trays instead of cells; a used takeout container with holes punched in the bottom makes a good nursery.

Take the fast route by sowing *sets*—essentially tiny, dime-sized onion bulbs. The rough-and-tumble early life of sets make them more prone to rot and problems than plants grown from seeds, but it's worth the small risk for a quick turnaround time. Plant transplants and sets outdoors when the soil is thawed enough to work, spacing them about 3" apart. Plant transplants ½" deep and sets an inch deep with the tip poking just above the soil.

Unlike onions, which produce one bulb per set, shallots grow in clusters, producing several bulbs from one set. Start them just like onions but provide a few more inches of space between sets.

Dig up onions whenever the fancy strikes. Both the green tops and young bulbs are tasty at any stage. Harvest full-sized storage onions and shallots when the tops start to brown and fall over. Stop watering them a week before the harvest date and hang the bulbs to cure, leaves and all, for several weeks.

WHAT'S THE DIFFERENCE?

Scallions, aka bunching onions, are varieties that mature into small bulbs no wider than the base of the leaves. Onions that are pulled while young and tender are often called scallions or green onions but are technically not the same thing.

Onions are divided into two camps: short day and long day. Choose short-day varieties in warm southern climates where the hours of day to night are more even, and choose long-day varieties in the north.

Peas

(Pisum sativum) — Legume Family (Leguminosae)

The best way to eat peas is straight off the plant as a crunchy, super fresh garden-side snack. Not a single pea makes it into my kitchen until I've finally grown exhausted of consuming them this way.

Good Growing

Like beans and other legumes, peas have the unique ability to make their own nitrogen, improving the soil along the way. Rotate them throughout your garden and peas will feed you and your soil year after year. Now that's multitasking! Peas grow best where the light is bright, but they will tolerate a little shade. Like just about every crop they benefit from good, rich soil with compost added at planting time. Spray young plants with liquid seaweed.

Pea plants are generally pretty easygoing with few problems. The biggest trouble tends to come from soggy soil, which leads to root or seed rot shortly after planting. Watch for puddling or heavy rain early on, and keep the soil consistently moist but not soggy. Hot weather is another big downer. Crops inevitably burn out as soon as the summer heat hits; however, getting started early, as soon as the ground can be worked, will help beat the heat a little. Shade covers also work in freak heat waves.

Peas are so much more than those mushy green bullets reviled by your little brother (and mine). Decorate your garden with varieties such as 'King Tut' and 'Blue Podded', all of which boast colorful, pendulous pods and flowers. I am fond of 'Laxton's Progress #9', whose flowers are so beautiful they can actually rival some ornamental (but inedible) sweet pea varieties. 'Mammoth Melting Sugar' is a sure hit if you like large, plump, and tender peas served plain or paired with mint and mashed into a pesto. Plant peas close to carrots, cucumber, spinach, radish, and parsley, but keep them away from the onion family.

GROWING IN POTS

Peas:
Suitability (Yield): Medium
Minimum Depth: 12"
Varieties: 'Carouby de Maussane', 'Golden Sweet'
More Tips: Stake large vines using sticks or poles fashioned into a tripod shape.

Dwarf Peas:
Suitability (Yield): High
Minimum Depth: 8"
Varieties: 'Dwarf Gray Sugar', 'Tom Thumb'
More Tips: Plant seeds 1" apart.

Fresh pea shoots are just as tasty as the pods. Snip a few off and enjoy raw in a leafy salad or as a crisp soup garnish.

Sowing and Planting

Peas grow best in the cooler ends of the season. As with beans, presoak hard peas overnight and dip the seeds in powdered *Rhizobia* bacteria before planting to increase crop yields. Direct-sow seeds outdoors as soon as the soil is thawed enough to dig. Take advantage of the cool late season and plant a second crop in late summer, about 3 months before the first frost. Sow dwarf varieties 1–2" apart and double the space for tall, vining plants.

Harvesting

Pinch off tender pods with your finger and cut off mature pods with scissors. Peas are in it for the long haul and will keep reproducing until the temperature gets too dang hot. Pods lose their sweetness if they're left on the plant too long, so check daily once they start to form. Pick snow peas when they are small and flat, and snap peas when the pods begin to swell. Shelling varieties should be plump yet still tender.

Clockwise from top left: Dip presoaked peas into *Rhizobia* bacteria immediately before planting; 'Blue Podded Shelling' is striking and edible; 'Golden Sweet' produces colorful peas and pinkish-purple flowers on gold-tinged vines. ▶

Peppers

(Capsicum) — Nightshade/Tomato Family (Solanaceae)

Fiery hot peppers invoke a sense of danger—too many in a meal can bring down an army. Not surprisingly, peppers, even the sweet varieties, are warm-weather plants that demand a long season. Don't let the limits of a cool or wet climate get in your way. Grow potted chilies indoors on a sunny windowsill and enjoy several seasons of spicy delights from the same plant!

Good Growing

All peppers need a long, warm growing season and a sunny spot. They prefer fertile soil but won't flower and set fruit if there is too much nitrogen. Peppers don't require a lot of water, but they are surprisingly picky about extreme temperatures. They like heat, but too much can cause plants to drop blossoms before setting fruit. Give the buds a dose of magnesium in the form of Epsom salt spray (page 77) to provide them a bit of liquid courage.

Grow sweet bell peppers in a rainbow of colors to liven up salads and pickles. 'Purple Beauty' bears fruit that start out and stay purple. 'King of the North' is a good choice in northern, short-season climates. There are almost no limits when it comes to hot peppers, with varieties that are pretty enough to steal the show in a flower garden and that bear fruit that isn't just hot but flavorful too. Connoisseurs of spice will favor varieties that rate high on the heat scale such as 'Fatali' and 'Habañero Brown'. To add a splash of life in dull spots, tuck in plants with variegated foliage such as 'Variegata' (aka 'Trifetti'), 'Chinese Five Color', 'Fish', and 'Golden Nugget'.

GROWING IN POTS

Container plants are susceptible to blossom-end rot. Provide more water during the fruiting and flowering stages.

Hot Peppers:
Suitability (Yield): High
Minimum Depth: 8"
Varieties: 'Chinese Ornamental', 'Cheyenne Orange Patio', 'Aurora'
More Tips: Bring small chili pepper plants indoors and grow as a houseplant in the sunniest window available.

Sweet Peppers:
Suitability (Yield): High
Minimum Depth: 8–12"
Varieties: 'Purple Beauty', 'Pepperoncini', 'Golden Treasure', 'Mohawk Gold Patio'

Clockwise from top left: 'Chinese Five ▶ Color' hot pepper is dramatic in a pot; bell peppers fit on a fire escape; three kinds of hot peppers just harvested; compact and ornamental (and edible) 'Variegata' hot pepper lends color to a small space.

Sowing and Planting

Sow pepper seeds indoors 6–8 weeks before the last frost. Keep seedlings in a warm spot with ample artificial light (16 hours/day) and wait until nighttime temperatures are above 55°F before planting them outdoors. Space large plants about 12" apart and grow only one plant per pot regardless of size. Plant them near basil, carrots, coriander, onions, and peas. Try not to follow with other plants in the tomato family.

Harvesting

Both hot and sweet peppers are prone to cycling through a variety of colors as they mature, although most can be harvested at any color. Sweet red peppers are sweeter and red hot peppers tend to be at their hottest, if left to fully develop. Consult the variety to determine final color. Twist or cut off the fruit when it is still firm. Don't wait for peppers to get floppy. Harvest everything before the first frost.

Making hotter hot peppers: Not all summers are created equal, and the change in climate from year to year can affect the quality of your harvest. Chili peppers thrive in hot summer sun, but will produce tasteless peppers during cooler, wet summers. Provide your plants with some tough love by moving them to the sunniest, brightest location possible and watering less often. A bit of drought will help crank the heat up.

Top down: 'Sweet Yellow Stuffing' peppers ▶ thrive in a 12"-deep container; Grow 'Chinese Ornamental' peppers on a sunny window ledge. Shown here in a 5" pot.

Tangy Red Pepper Ketchup

My gang *loves* this ketchup, and that's saying a lot because we are die-hard mustard people. It is so tangy, tasty, and versatile that you'll be adding a dab to everything before you know it. And then throw out the mediocre store-bought brand because that tired relationship is over.

1. Finely chop the sweet peppers, onion, and apples in a food processor and transfer to a medium cooking pot.

2. Add the vinegar, salt, honey, molasses, and lemon slices. Stir until well mixed.

3. To make the spice packet, cut a 5" square of cheesecloth. Place the ingredients in the center of the square; pull up the sides and tie closed with a piece of cotton twine. Submerge in the sauce.

4. Turn the heat up high and bring the ingredients to a boil. Reduce the heat to medium and simmer uncovered for 40 minutes, until wet and syrupy. Stir occasionally to prevent the ingredients from sticking or burning on the bottom.

5. Discard the lemon slices and reduce the heat to low. Continue simmering for another 40 minutes, or until the mix is thick and sticky.

6. Discard the spice packet. Press the mixture through a food mill to make a smooth sauce.

7. If it still seems too watery, put it back on the stove and simmer over medium-low heat until the ketchup has reduced and thickened to a consistency that suits you.

8. Pour into sterilized jars, leaving ½" headspace, and process in a boiling-water bath for 15 minutes. Detailed canning instructions can be found starting on page 189.

Makes approximately 11 quarter-pint jars

- 3 pounds red sweet peppers, cored, sliced, and cut into large chunks
- 1 large onion, cut into large chunks
- 2 apples, cored and cut into large chunks
- 1½ cups apple cider vinegar
- 1 teaspoon coarse salt
- 1½ cups honey
- 1 tablespoon blackstrap molasses
- ½ lemon, sliced

SPICE PACKET:
- 1 tablespoon whole black peppercorns
- 2 tablespoons mustard seed
- 1 tablespoon coriander seed

Root Vegetables

Poor, overlooked root vegetables. I'll admit that even I forget about growing them most of the time, yet growing root vegetables is actually quite a treat. You can watch the development of most veggies firsthand, but root veggies are a surprise—you never know what you're going to dig up, and they're always sweeter and fresher than you remembered!

Good Growing

Most root vegetables are cold-weather crops, which is a nice bonus because getting them in the ground early means you'll be eating from the garden before the tomatoes have set roots. Most require similar growing conditions and are generally unfussy, light feeders. They all grow best in full sun but will tolerate light shade. It's a good idea to add lots of compost in early spring to make that well-draining soil they like. Underground rocks will get in their way and create some roots gnarly enough to be worthy of an entry in the Most Deformed Vegetable category, so it's worth pulling out even the small stones or growing the vegetables in a raised bed.

All but Jerusalem artichokes hate extreme heat, so be sure to mulch in the summer with something loose and spreadable like grass clippings to cool things down and lock in moisture. Stress caused by underwatering and heat is the most common cause of lackluster root crops, as are pesky carrot flies and flea beetles.

GROWING IN POTS

Beet:
Suitability (Yield): High
Minimum Depth: 10–12"
Varieties: 'Baby Ball', 'Cylindra'

Carrot:
Suitability (Yield): High
Minimum Depth: 10–12"
Varieties: 'Danver's Half Long', 'Round Romeo', 'Thumbelina'

Jerusalem Artichoke:
Suitability (Yield): Medium
Minimum Depth: 16"
More Tips: Plant a handful in a plastic garbage bin.

Potatoes:
See "Trash Can Spuds" (page 112).

Radish:
Suitability (Yield): Medium
Minimum Depth: 6"
Varieties: 'Cherry Belle', brightly blushed 'Purple Plum'
More Tips: Great for window box growing.

Beet

(Beta vulgaris) — Beet Family (Chenopodiaceae)

Although the root is the main event, the bold beet leaves make a great statement in the garden and are available in a wide palette of colors including yellow, red-veined, and deep burgundy. 'Bull's Blood' stands out the most, but there are lots of gorgeous varieties to consider, including 'Chioggia', whose red-and-white-striped rings resemble a bull's-eye, and the mild flavor of 'Burpee's Golden'.

Beet seeds are actually clusters of several seeds stuck together. Plant them outdoors just before carrots, 2–4 weeks before the last frost. Thin out seedlings (see page 29), allowing 3–4" between plants to accommodate root growth. Add the tender young castaways to salads—nothing goes to waste! Tough, mature greens are best served cooked. In the garden, pair with cabbage, lettuce, onion, and radish, but keep away from beans, Swiss chard, and spinach.

Begin harvesting when the roots are 2" wide. Pull or dig them out carefully and twist off the leafy tops.

Carrot

(Daucus carota) — Carrot Family (Apiaceae)

Surprise yourself come harvest time by growing a mix of colorful carrots including the nuclear 'Atomic Red', the ghostly 'Belgian White', or the Jimi Hendrix–approved 'Purple Haze'.

Sow seeds outdoors about ½" deep when the soil starts to warm up, about 2–3 weeks before the last frost. Be patient—carrots are notoriously slow to germinate. Thin out small seedlings (see page 29) to 2–3" between plants.

Carrots are ready to eat at any size. Simply yank them up by the leaves or loosen first with a shovel. Harvest storage carrots just before the first frost date.

Carrots are fast friends with lettuce, members of the onion family, peas, and tomatoes. Carrot cousins, including dill and parsnip, should be grown elsewhere.

Jerusalem Artichoke

(Helianthus tuberosus) — Aster/Composite Family (Asteraceae)

Jerusalem artichoke, aka sunchoke, is a classic "hippie" staple that is gaining mainstream attention. The flowers, which bloom in late summer on 7- to 10-foot stalks, resemble small sunflowers but underneath the ground the plant produces crisp, nutty-tasting, knobby tubers. Incredibly easy to grow, sunchokes thrive in the worst conditions and can actually run riot in the ground if not reined in. Before rushing out to buy some, be forewarned that the taste, though loved by many, isn't for everyone. Buy a mature choke from your local health food store and give it a taste before committing to a crop—a single plant can produce a lot of tubers! And to put it delicately, the tuber hasn't earned the nickname "fartichoke" for nothing.

In midspring, plant whole or chopped tubers (follow the directions for preparing potato seeds on page 112) 3"–6" deep with a good 20" between each. They're not heavy drinkers and can be virtually left alone all summer long.

A kiss of cold sweetens tubers; dig them out of the soil in late autumn just after a hard frost.

◀ Clockwise from top left: Jerusalem artichokes are easygoing both in-ground and in big pots; picky eaters are more likely to try colorful carrots; cheerful 'Chioggia' beet will brighten up your dinner plate; 'French Breakfast' radishes are ready to harvest in 30 days.

Potatoes

(*Solanum tuberosum*) — Nightshade/Tomato Family (Solanaceae)

Potatoes hate extremes and will not tolerate cold, wet conditions, or extremely high heat. The plants aren't generally attractive; however, some varieties, including 'Purple Peruvian', 'Red Cloud', and 'Cranberry Red', feature colorful flowers.

Sow seed potatoes approximately 2 weeks before the last frost, or when the soil temperature is above 45°F. Feel free to plant seed potatoes that have already sprouted. In fact, some gardeners intentionally presprout before planting, placing "seeds" in a cool, dry location to "chit."

The size of mature potatoes depends on how closely you plant seeds—the closer you plant, the smaller the potatoes. Sow them 6–15" apart in a shallow trench about 3" deep. Bush beans, peas, marigolds, and cabbage make good companions; however, potatoes do not grow well with members of the cucumber and tomato families.

Once plants have grown 8–12" tall, mound soil up around the stems, leaving about a third of the plant above. This is called *hilling*. You can go freeform or create supports using bottomless boxes made from recycled wood or tires, stacking up layers and adding in new soil until flowers appear.

Harvest "new" potatoes a few months after planting by lifting the entire plant out of the soil. To harvest mature, storage potatoes, leave plants untouched until late summer or early fall. Sometime after flowering, the potato leaves will begin to yellow and wither. Once this happens, stop watering for about two weeks and allow nature to take its course.

Spread storage potatoes out on a pad of newspapers in a cool, dry place. In a couple of days they'll be ready to brush clean and put away for the long haul.

Radish

(*Raphanus sativus*) — Cabbage Family (Cruciferae)

Despite their tough exterior, radishes are a sensitive root veg that needs more water than other root vegetables. This fact alone made it my nemesis in the container garden until a few years ago, when I finally found the perfect balance and a few varieties that were right for the job. Elegantly long and bicolored 'French Breakfast' is a perennial favorite, and 'Black Spanish Round' is spicy and unique.

Radishes are one of the first seeds I sow outdoors both in the ground and in containers just as soon as the soil has thawed enough to dig. Sow seeds in rows or tuck them into empty spaces between other plants, spacing 1–2" apart and ½" deep. They're a great pest repellent for the squash family. Through the spring and then again in fall, replace any plants you pull with a fresh seed to ensure a regular harvest. Give it a break during the warm months. Instead, grow 'Rat-Tailed Radish' (*Raphanus sativus* 'Caudatus'), an Asian heirloom that produces spicy radish-flavored seedpods instead of roots.

Pull out radish roots when they are an inch wide or as soon as the shoulders show above the soil. Allow forgotten roots to grow light and peppery-tasting flowers for salads, but don't bother with eating the husky root at that point.

RECIPE
Root Vegetable Fries

Roasted potatoes are good and all, but a roasted root vegetable medley is just as easy to make and a little bit fancy too. Substitute any root vegetable, including starchy potatoes, turnip, parsnip, celery root, or rutabaga. While the veggies are roasting, toss a garlic bulb or two into the pan at about the 30-minute mark—the result: easy, creamy garlic! Yum.

1. Preheat the oven to 400°F. Cut the vegetables into ½"-wide spears and toss in a roasting pan with olive oil and herbs to coat. Keep the peels on; that's where the vitamins are.

2. Roast for approximately 40 minutes, turning regularly until all sides have turned a golden brown and the fries are cooked straight through.

3. Serve with Tangy Red Pepper Ketchup (page 105) or splash on one of the Herb and Flower Vinegars (page 196) for a high-falutin' version of the classic chip-wagon fry.

Serves 2–4

- 1 large carrot
- 1 large potato
- 1 large sweet potato
- 1 large beet
- 2 tablespoons olive oil
- 1 teaspoon chopped fresh thyme
- ½ teaspoon chopped fresh rosemary
- Salt and pepper

Trash Can Spuds

Technically speaking, potatoes aren't roots but tubers, bulbous growths (tasty, tasty growths) that actually develop off the stem. Container-grown potatoes develop in an interesting way, producing a vine above the soil surface that likes to have soil mounded up the sides as it grows. Wrapping your brain around the backward logic of starting spuds in the bottom of a large container will make sense come fall when you are digging out piles of tasty taters for the best carb meal ever.

CHOOSING A CONTAINER

Any old trash can will do, whether it is made of plastic or galvanized metal. The *Sesame Street* look of a metal bin may be more your style, but bear in mind that in the scorching sun the heat-absorbing properties of metal can roast growing spuds before their time.

YOU WILL NEED

- A drill and a ½" drill bit or a large nail
- A large garbage can (minimum 18" deep)
- Three bricks or two 1" × 4" boards
- Container soil
- Seed potatoes

Preparing Seed Potatoes: Plant small seed potatoes whole. Large tubers will need to be chopped up into chunks about 1½" thick. Set chunks aside to heal for a few days to prevent rotting.

1. Using a drill or large nail, make several holes in the bottom of the garbage can. I suggest at least ten holes to cover a surface area approximately 15" wide. Add extra holes to the sides of your bin to reduce the risk of rotting in very wet and rainy locations. Evenly distribute the bricks under the can as props to facilitate better drainage. Wood boards or cement blocks will work just as well—anything to keep the bin from sitting in a pool of water.

2. Fill the can with 6" of container soil. Spread chunks or whole seed potatoes evenly over the surface with 5–6" between them. Cover with 2–3" of soil and water in lightly. Keep the soil adequately moist (but not soaking), and within a few days you should notice shoots peeking up through the soil. Amazing, ain't it?

3. When plant stems have grown about 8" high, add handfuls of soil to the bin until about two-thirds of the plants are covered. Repeat this process until the plants reach the top of the bin and begin to flower. Get excited! Keep your plants watered during this period so that the soil is moist but not soggy. For more growing tips, see "Potatoes" on page 110.

4. When your plants have finished flowering, they will start to turn yellow and die. Cut back on watering significantly, allowing the vines to dry out.

5. Within a few weeks, once the vines have withered, harvest your reward by either tipping the can over and allowing the goods to spill out or, for a cleaner method, digging the spuds out with a shovel. Pat yourself on the back, then hurry and get those babies ready for eating.

The entire procedure from start to finish should take 65–100 days.

1

2

4

Summer and Winter Squash

Complaining about too much squash is a gardener's rite of passage, especially when it comes to zucchini, also known as summer squash—a single plant can bury you in produce almost overnight. But I'm not complaining! Bring it on! On the other hand, slow-growing winter squash are a tease, taking what feels like ages before they reach maturity. But it's worth having patience. These vegetables are built to last, enduring months and months with hardly any effort or special consideration at all.

Good Growing

Both summer and winter squash are voracious plants, greedy for all the sun, water, and soil nutrition you can give them. Zucchini are the less demanding of the two, growing smaller plants and fruit that give as good as they get and finish their business just as winter squashes are revving their engines.

Unfortunately a lot of pests and diseases are jockeying for a chance to get at your squash before you do. It's not you; it's them! Prune out a few leaves as plants develop to reduce humidity and prevent disease. Look out for squash vine borer, cucumber beetle, squash bugs, and aphids. Grow squash near basil, beans, nasturtium, onions, and radish but do not follow with other cucurbits. You might try a good-weather dance while you're at it.

All squash plants, regardless of type, are space hogs—give each plant a bit of room whether in the ground or in pots. The trailing types will probably end up in a tangled mess regardless of how much room is provided. Go ahead and stake them up on a strong and sturdy trellis if you prefer a neat and tidy garden.

Start seeds indoors 2–4 weeks before the last frost in order to get a head start on the growing season. It is generally safe to move your plants outdoors 2 weeks after the last frost date in your area, but if the weather is iffy give it an extra week. When it comes time to plant them in the garden, make a mound of compost on top of the soil, about a foot in diameter, and place two or three plants within the mound. Set a plastic bottle with the bottom cut off over young transplants to protect them from unexpected cold snaps.

GROWING IN POTS

Choose large and extra-large bins—yep, even for the bushing types; these plants don't mess around! The bigger the pot, the happier your plant and the better your harvest.

Summer Squash (Bush):
Suitability (Yield): Medium
Minimum Depth: 10–12"
Varieties: Compact heirlooms such as 'Wood's Prolific Scallop' and 'Ronde de Nice'; smaller hybrids such as 'Spacemiser' and 'Sunburst'

Winter Squash and Pumpkin:
Suitability (Yield): Low
Minimum Depth: 14–16"
Varieties: 'Table Bush Queen', 'Delicata', 'Cheyenne Bush' (pumpkin)
More Tips: Self-watering containers will help regulate soil moisture over 4 months of growing. See "Set It and Forget It (Well, Almost)" (page 54).

Clockwise from top left: Pluck pattypan and 'Golden Acorn' squash while they are small and tender; 'Butternut' is a popular winter storage squash; Grow 'Ronde de Nice' zucchini in a large pot; 'Turk's Turban' winter squash.

Pollination Problems

Squash, cucumbers, and melons all produce distinctly male and female flowers on the same plant rather than packing all the parts into one flower. If you find your plant producing lots of flowers but no fruit, you'll need to stage an intervention. Allow me to school you in Flower Sex Ed 101. The female flower produces fruit and is distinguished by a micro squash that sits just behind the petals waiting to be fertilized by pollen from the male flower. Pick a male flower (identified by a straight stem behind the petals) and gently peel off the outer petals to expose the pollen. Brush the pollen lightly onto the female flower parts. Congratulations; you've just made a baby zucchini!

Plants typically put out a bunch of male flowers early on before the females finally make an appearance. Don't worry; you'll have plenty of time to grow fruit. In the meantime, pluck off the flowers when they are just opened and eat them with dinner. Stuffed squash blossoms are the best—they're even better than the fruit. Stuff them with cheese and herbs, dip them in a little batter, and pan-fry until crispy. Heaven!

Summer Squash

(*Cucurbita pepo*) — Cucurbit Family (Cucurbitaceae)

Zucchini is by far the easiest and most productive squash type to grow in a small garden. It's a versatile vegetable that comes in an array of shapes, sizes, and colors, including the usual cylindrical-shaped green type, white, yellow, crookneck, round, and scallop-shaped. The plants themselves come in two forms, bush and trailing, the former being best suited for small spaces and ample-sized pots that are at least 15" deep. 'Costata Romanesco' is a favorite heirloom with beautiful leaves and fruit that

grows into a beast—albeit a delicious one—seemingly overnight.

Baby zucchinis grow fast and furiously; twist them off when they are 3–6" at the most. Smaller zucchinis taste better, and regular picking ensures a continuing harvest up to the end of summer.

Winter Squash and Pumpkin

(*Cucurbita moschata* and *Cucurbita maxima*) — Cucurbit Family (Cucurbitaceae)

Winter squash are monsters, growing larger plants and fruit than their summer cousins, meaning that they are more demanding all around, especially in the water department. They also require high nutrition and are known to thrive best growing straight out of the compost bin. If you've got full sun on your bin, why not give it a try?

Loads of winter squash varieties are available in all sorts of colors and gnarled, bumpy shapes. The acorn squash is classic, but why do we always fall back on it when so many others are waiting to be tried? If you've got the space, live dangerously and grow a crop of something fabulously ugly/beautiful like 'Marina di Chioggia', 'Black Futsu', or 'Musquee de Provence'.

Prop young, developing fruit off the ground on top of bricks, overturned pots, plastic containers, or metal cans to keep them rot-free and safe from pests. Start looking for signs of ripeness in late summer or early fall. Harvest when the plants have died back and the skin is too hard to dent with your nail. Keep the squash on the plant until fully mature to ensure good storage ability.

Roasted Zucchini Dip

Once or twice per season, a zucchini is lost in the tangle of leaves or just plain forgotten and I get stuck with the squash that ate Manhattan. A vegetable that hard, dry, and wooden does not seem fit to eat, yet the thought of throwing it into the bin seems just plain wrong. In the quest to make the inedible delicious, this recipe was born.

Serve this dip with chopped vegetables cut into long strips or with chips or crackers. It is also delicious spread on bread as an alternative to traditional condiments.

1. Preheat the oven to 400°F. Place the zucchini, onion, and bell pepper in a roasting pan, peels and all. Drizzle the oil over the vegetables, sprinkle them with the salt, and roast for 45 minutes, turning everything over halfway through cooking.

2. Set aside to cool for 15 minutes.

3. Separate the charred peels from the soft flesh of the vegetables and discard. Place the vegetables in the food processor. Add the remaining ingredients and pulse until smooth.

4. Chill and serve.

   Makes 2–3 cups

- 1 monster zucchini (1½–2 pounds), cut in half
- 1 small onion, cut in half
- 1 red or green bell pepper, cut in half
- 1 tablespoon olive oil
- Pinch of salt
- 1 garlic clove
- 1 tablespoon lemon juice
- 1 teaspoon fresh or dried oregano
- 1 small hot pepper, or to taste

Super Easy Veggie Stock

I can't stand most store-bought stock. That stuff tastes odd to me—too salty and never like the ingredients listed. But a little stock in soups and stews is so much better than water. Fortunately, homemade stock is pretty easy to make. It's also a really good way to squeeze just a little bit more from your homegrown produce. Use up asparagus ends, leek greens, corncobs with the kernels removed, and the parsley that is taking over the garden.

Just about anything that is fit for consumption can go into a stock, barring a few exceptions like cabbage, cauliflower, broccoli, and beets, whose flavors are just too intense. Remember that we're not making water into wine here—keep old, rotten, or garbage parts out and throw them in the compost bin instead.

1. Wash and coarsely chop the vegetables and herbs. Leave the herb stems intact, but remove vegetable peels.

2. Toss everything into a large or small stockpot (depending on quantities) and add enough water to cover.

3. Bring to a boil, then reduce heat and simmer for 1 hour.

4. Strain the cooked stock through a colander. Pour the liquid gold into jars and chuck the plant bits into the compost bin. Keep the stock in the fridge for immediate use or freeze for long-term storage.

INGREDIENTS FOR STOCK

VEGETABLES

- Onions
- Garlic
- Leeks
- Carrots
- Celery
- Lettuce
- Tomato
- Green beans
- Sweet potato
- Parsnip
- Asparagus stems
- Squash
- Peas
- Corncobs
- Shallots
- Swiss chard

HERBS

- Chives
- Thyme
- Parsley
- Marjoram
- Rosemary
- Basil

Swiss Chard

(*Beta vulgaris* Cicla Group) — Beet Family (Chenopodiaceae)

Swiss chard is a looker with big, wrinkly leaves in gorgeous luminescent colors. But the real magic of Swiss chard is that it can sustain itself quite easily just about anywhere with hardly any effort at all. You're missing out on a lot of easy eats if you're not growing it already.

Good Growing

Swiss chard loves a sunny spot in the garden, although it will tolerate some shade. It's not a particularly heavy feeder but will perform at its best in rich soil with good drainage. Light, monthly applications of fish emulsion and seaweed will bring out those lush leaves and make them shine brightly.

Swiss chard is also known as "perpetual spinach" in some countries because of its ability to resist bolting in the heat yet endure a light freeze. An infestation of flea beetles will diminish its beauty, but the real kicker is leafminer, which can be beat if you remove the infested leaves quickly and regularly. Disease and pest problems are often the result of a lack of sun or proper root space. Grow Swiss chard with the cabbage family, lettuce, borage, and beans, but keep it away from beets and spinach.

Traditional white-stemmed Swiss chard is nice, but 'Bright Lights' and 'Five Color Silverbeet' are particularly striking.

Sowing and Planting

Direct-sow seeds outdoors 2 weeks before the last frost. Alternatively, start seeds in toilet paper rolls (see "Toilet Roll Seed-Starting Cells," page 27), and transplant into the garden, spacing plants about 8" apart.

Harvesting

Swiss chard is good at any size, so the best time to harvest is really a matter of taste. If you prefer young chard, clip the leaves ½" above the soil when they're only a few inches tall. Harvest larger leaves and crunchy stems just as you would lettuce, leaving the root and 2" of stem intact.

GROWING IN POTS

Grow in smaller pots when growing immature plants for salad greens.

Swiss Chard:
Suitability (Yield): High
Minimum Depth: 10"
Varieties: All; 'Pot of Gold', 'Rhubarb', 'Golden'
More Tips: Mature plants produce deep roots that will quickly fill the pot they are planted in.

Tomatoes

(Lycopersicon esculentum) — Nightshade/Tomato Family (Solanaceae)

How do I introduce the best homegrown food crop in the whole world? The pungent smell of tomato seedlings lined up on the windowsill has come to represent that first gleeful glimpse of spring, and it never fails to make me squeal like a preteen. If, say by some cruel twist of fate, I were forced to choose one plant to grow for the rest of my life, I would pick tomatoes. And I would still die happy.

Good Growing

Tomatoes are sun worshippers that need 6 hours of direct sun per day; don't even try to mess with this. They just won't produce in shadier spots. Fertile, well-draining soil is a must, although I have discovered wild types growing in shockingly derelict conditions.

Regardless of size, tomatoes are superproducers—this kind of effort can really wipe a plant out! Give them a lot of nitrogen early in the season while plants are making leaves and stems. Too much nitrogen can result in a lush plant that never produces fruit, however. And we want fruit! When the blossoms show up, cut back on nitrogen and keep adding potassium every 2 weeks.

How you water tomatoes is as important as how much you give them. Getting the leaves wet when there is a lack of proper airflow around the plants invites all kinds of fungal and viral diseases to take hold. Tomato plants especially dislike high humidity but require a long drink now and again. The trick is to water heavily but infrequently, concentrating the flow at the soil. Water your plants more often during heat waves and long periods of drought, but always provide a long drink every single time. Using mulch around the plants will help lock in moisture and prevent water from splashing up onto lower leaves.

GROWING IN POTS

Water container-grown plants every day (more in a heat wave).

Tomato (Indeterminates):
Suitability (Yield): Medium
Minimum Depth: 16–18"
Varieties: 'Black Krim', 'Zapotec Pink Pleated', Brandywine', 'Purple Calabash'
More Tips: Grow one plant per pot regardless of the size of the pot or plant. Tomatoes are naturally large-rooted plants; your strategy to double the harvest will only result in two unhealthy plants and no harvest. In a big tub, grow tomatoes with basil, flowers, or lettuce.

Tomato (Determinate and Semideterminate):
Suitability (Yield): Medium-high
Minimum Depth: 12"
Varieties: 'Whippersnapper', 'Green Grape', 'Black Seaman', 'Silver Fir Tree'

Tomato (Dwarf Hybrid):
Suitability (Yield): High
Minimum Depth: 6"
Varieties: 'Tiny Tim', 'Toy Boy'

'Purple Calabash' has a rich, tangy ▶ flavor that makes a delicious sauce.

All tomato plants are not created equal. They have been categorized by growth habit as a way to get a better handle on the zillions of existing varieties. Understanding these differences right off the bat will really help you choose a tomato that is right for your growing conditions and desires. Also, keep in mind that the size of a plant does not always determine the size of the fruit. Some gigantic plants grow teeny little tomatoes, and some small plants grow fist-sized slicers. For this reason, understanding categories is important, but so is getting the scoop on each variety before planting a seed.

Indeterminates are the granddaddies of the tomato world. They grow into massive vines and keep producing fruit until the frost puts an end to things. Many of the most delicious varieties are indeterminates, which is why we all want to grow them. Container gardeners should go with extra-large bins for the best harvest.

Determinates are smaller bushing plants that max out their growth at a certain point and produce fruit all at once.

Semideterminates stop their growth like a determinate but produce another crop like an indeterminate.

Dwarf hybrids are diminutive plants that always grow cherry-sized fruit. They are the best option in hanging baskets and window boxes.

Consistent soil moisture is also important in preventing blossom-end rot (page 72). Watch moisture levels while fruit is ripening—a heavy hand with the hose can cause mushy, mealy fruit that split.

Take the opportunity during watering to inspect the nooks and crannies for tomato hornworm, aphids, slugs, and symptoms of disease.

Despite the tomato's reputation as a sun worshipper, extremely high summer temperatures can cause tomato blossoms to drop before setting fruit. Sometimes it's just a matter of waiting out a heat wave; the plants will bounce back and start producing fruit as soon as the temperature drops. You can always try draping shade covers over plants in extreme cases or apply Epsom salt spray (page 77) to new blossoms.

Sowing and Planting

Start tomato seeds indoors 6–8 weeks before the last frost. The seedlings can generally go out about a week after the last frost, but watch the weather and protect plants with a miniature greenhouse or cloche in the event of a fluke cold snap. Tomatoes grow roots all along their stem, providing an assortment of ways to plant seedlings. You can either plant deeply, burying the stem vertically in the soil, or make a shallow trench and plant the stem lying down horizontally. Either method works well and results in a sturdy, healthy root system, but the horizontal method makes use of the upper layer of soil, which is warmed by the sun's heat earlier in the season. On the other hand, the horizontal method makes it hard to protect the stem from cutworms using a cutworm collar (page 75). Whichever method you use, be sure to strip the lower leaves first, keeping just the top cluster above the ground. Add a little vermicompost or compost to the hole before filling in with soil.

Tomatoes welcome companionship in the ground and in pots alongside basil, borage, gem marigolds, lettuce, calendula, nasturtium, the cabbage family, and the onion family. Keep away from dill, fennel, and potato.

Stake tall varieties before or right after planting to avoid the risk of hurting established roots later on. Staking isn't absolutely necessary; however, staked plants can be grown 2' apart, but sprawling plants need double the legroom.

My preferred staking method in a small space is to sink four stakes into the ground in a square formation and tie or wire at the top like a tripod or tepee, growing one plant up each side. This seems to use space efficiently and looks a bit neater than rows of poles sticking out like gravestones. As the plants grow, loosely tie their vines to the stake using string, twine, or strips of ripped T-shirt and panty hose.

Pruning

Staked plants need pruning early in the growing season; this process directs the growth into a single main stem that will eventually produce plump and juicy fruit. Pinch off all of the lower growth as well as new stems called *suckers* that come up between branches, keeping leaves at the top to feed the plant and provide shade.

The first hard frost in fall will kill off any plants that have been left in the soil. In climates with shorter seasons, you're better off pruning back the tops of indeterminates toward the end of summer to focus any remaining energy and time into growing the remaining fruit.

Harvesting

You'll know when your tomatoes are ready because they'll have reached their mature color, be soft to the touch, and taste oh-so-delicious on a sandwich.

The tripod staking method works with ▶ containers too, but stick to one plant per pot. The tall indeterminate 'Black Brandywine' is shown here growing in a deep metal garbage can alongside purple shiso and marigolds.

Smoky 'Black Plum' Tomato Sauce

This is the yummiest and most effortless tomato sauce you will ever make, hands down. Roasting the tomatoes in the oven allows the juices to caramelize, creating a sauce that is sweet and rich. 'Black Plum' is the best variety for the job. It has a built-in smoky richness that is enhanced when the tomatoes are roasted. Don't be afraid to substitute any plum tomato variety—they all taste great done up this way.

- 5 pounds 'Black Plum' tomatoes
- 2 tablespoons olive oil
- 1 teaspoon sea salt
- 4 large fresh basil leaves, optional
- 3 garlic cloves, optional

1. Preheat the oven to 400°F. Put the whole tomatoes into a roasting pan.

2. Drizzle the oil over the tomatoes and sprinkle them with the salt. Tuck the basil leaves and garlic, if using, between the tomatoes, where they will stay moist in the juices that will be released.

3. Place the pan on the middle rack and roast for 30–40 minutes, or until the tomato skins have blackened a bit.

4. Set the pan aside to cool for 20 minutes. Careful, roasted tomatoes are hot!

5. Stand a food mill or old-fashioned chinois (a metal cone sieve with wooden pestle) over a large bowl and work the cooked tomatoes through, a few at a time, discarding the seeds and skins.

6. Use right away or keep in the fridge up to a week.

Makes about 5 cups

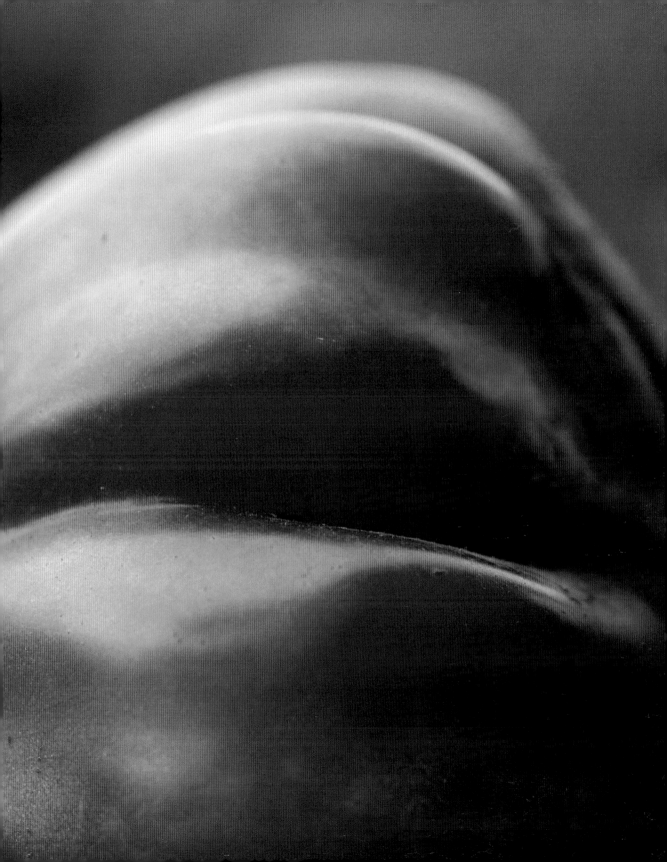

Upside-Down Tomatoes

As a microspace gardener I'm always looking for ways to fit in one more plant, either that tomato I couldn't bear to part with or the 'Cinnamon' basil I just had to have. Growing a tomato or hot pepper plant upside down saves space, makes care and maintenance easier, and, some say, even increases the yield—no staking required! I always manage to find room on top for a basil plant too. Crisis averted.

CHOOSING A CONTAINER
Stick to deep buckets with a strong metal handle; plastic handles can't bear the weight. An old bucket with a mop-wringing contraption does double duty by maintaining the bucket's shape and adding an extra tier for planting.

CHOOSING A TOMATO PLANT
The size of your bucket will determine the type of tomato plant you can grow; however, plants that are small to medium-sized at maturity with cherry-sized fruit are your best bet.

Try: 'Peacevine Cherry', 'Gold Rush Currant', or a wild variety such as 'Cheeseman's' or 'Matt's Wild Cherry'.

YOU WILL NEED
- A bucket with a metal handle
- A drill and a 2" drill bit
- Scissors
- Coir lining
- Tomato seedling
- Potting soil
- Two or three basil plants (shown: 'Purple Ruffles' and 'Pesto Perpetuo')

1. You will require a place to hang your upside-down tomato about midway through preparing the bucket, so it's smart to have that place ready before getting started. Once it's filled with soil, your upside-down planter is going to be very heavy, so be sure to choose a location that is sturdy and can hold the weight.

2. Drill a hole in the bottom of the bucket with a 2" drill bit.

3. Use scissors to cut a piece of coir lining into a 5" circle. Cut a slit in the center. This will hold the plant in place until it grows roots and will prevent soil from falling out the hole in the bucket.

4. Turn the bucket over and gently push the seedling's root ball through the hole as if to plant it.

5. Turn the bucket over so that the inside is facing right side up again while holding the plant in place. Holding the piece of coir, open the slit and wrap it around the stem of the seedling. Close the slit. This should grip the tomato stem and hold it in place inside the bucket.

6. Hang the bucket and fill it with potting soil.

7. Plant the top with basil or another shallow-rooted herb. Planting the top keeps the soil cool and looks pretty too.

CHAPTER 8:

Fruit

Despite our wishful thinking, conventionally grown fruit never compares to the real deal. It's often bland, always sprayed, and never fresh. I grew up in a fruit-farming region, but it took growing my own to have a religious experience with a strawberry.

You can't exactly wash pesticides off the delicate, textured skins of berries. The residue is there forever, either on the skin or in the soil. I worked as a fruit-picking day worker one summer during my early adolescence, and the worst part wasn't falling off ladders or backbreaking hours bent down low, but the pesticides. The trees, plants, and fruit were thick with it. I've never forgotten that smell or the feeling of it on my skin.

I've tried to talk myself out of growing fruit countless times, claiming I don't have the space, know-how, or time. All of those excuses are forgotten the moment that first ripe fruit comes in. Homegrown fruit never, ever disappoints.

Fruit-bearing plants come in all shapes and sizes, from little plants to massive trees and everything in between. They also hail from different climates. Knowing the origin of your crop and how it grows in the wild can provide some insight into how to make it happy in the garden. Most fruit comes from perennial plants that will last in your garden for years, so it is in your best interest to consider the health of your plants over both the short and long term. Regular weekly care as well as yearly maintenance, including pruning and soil building, guarantees a good return on your investment and a better harvest to come.

Just like vegetables, fruit-producing plants will be happiest and grow the juiciest crop when they've got room to breathe. When growing potted crops, look for dwarf varieties that produce smaller fruit and don't skimp on the size of the pot. Repot into slightly larger containers every couple of years and replenish the soil yearly.

Pop jewel-like kumquats into your mouth ▶
whole (rind and all) or add to a martini
as an unusual olive replacement. The
compact trees are ideally suited to growing
in small spaces or medium-sized pots.

Blueberries

(Vaccinium corymbosum) — Heath Family (Ericaceae)

If you've got the space, blueberry bushes make a gorgeous edible hedge with leaves that take on stunning red hues in the fall. If not, you can still grow a couple of plants in containers. The really tall highbush plants need a fairly big pot, but the roots are shallow and the plant is tough enough to withstand life on a roof. You'll be able to harvest your berries for decades to come!

Good Growing

In the wild, blueberries are most often found growing on the edges of coniferous forests, which should say a lot about the kind of soil and conditions they prefer. They're one of the few edibles that thrive in acidic soil, which is good news if you've got a pine tree in your yard that nothing will grow near. Blueberry plants like full sun with soil that retains moisture well, yet is also well draining. Confusing, I know. But think of the soil you'll find in a coniferous forest: really light and airy but rich in organic matter from fallen leaves and needles. The berry plants will tolerate partial shade but produce bigger harvests in the sunniest spots that have a bit of wind coverage.

Prune plants in late summer or early spring while they are still dormant. Blueberries yield on younger branches, so prune out any growth that is over 5 years old as well as diseased, broken, and dead branches. Remove some bushiness from the center to discourage fungal problems.

Sowing and Planting

Plant dormant bushes in very early spring as soon as the soil can be worked. Plant in the late fall in mild climates. Add lots of compost and organic matter to the soil at planting time. Highbush plants need at least 6' of padding from other plants, but lowbush can be planted as close as 2' apart. Dig a hole that is the same depth as the plant's pot and water in well.

Blueberries are self-pollinating, but they don't do it very successfully. You'll get the best crops if you grow at least one other variety to promote cross-pollination. Pick the flowers off

---

GROWING IN POTS

Blueberries need a cold climate, yet their shallow roots are susceptible to freezing in pots over very cold winters. Choose cold-hardy varieties.

Blueberries:
Suitability (Yield): High
Minimum Depth: 16–20"
Varieties: 'Blueray', 'Northland', 'Patriot', 'Top Hat' (compact dwarf for warm climates)
More Tips: To overwinter pots, wrap with burlap and place in a sheltered spot or store in a cold shed.

in the first few years, if you can stand to do it, so the plant can put energy into growing healthy roots. This may seem like a drag, but it will lead to better harvests down the road—one plant can keep producing for decades. As a bonus, container-grown plants can always move with you.

Harvesting

Different varieties are ready at slightly different times; however, most tend to ripen around midsummer. Don't harvest the berries the minute they turn blue. Wait 3–6 more days for the best flavor.

WHAT'S THE DIFFERENCE?

Blueberry bushes are categorized by height.

Lowbush blueberries (*Vaccinium angustifolium*) are a short and small wild type commonly found growing on the edge of northern coniferous forests. They stay under 2' tall.

Highbush plants are large, cultivated bushes, although some do grow wild. They sometimes grow up to 13' tall! Half-high bushes fall somewhere in between the two.

Very northern, cold-climate gardeners are best off growing cold-hardy lowbush or half-highbush plants. Only a few highbush varieties are tough enough.

Citrus Containers

Variegated 'Centennial' kumquat makes an attractive, yet edible houseplant.

Perhaps I'm just a cold-climate pessimist, but before I tried growing citrus indoors in a pot, I was absolutely convinced that the prospect of doing so was some kind of mean-spirited joke perpetuated by the fortunate few who have their own greenhouses. I'm not going to pretend it's easy, but having grown several I can say it certainly is doable—and a lot of fun!

Citrus trees have shallow, wide root systems, making them excellent candidates for container growing, especially in cold climates. There are plenty of small and dwarf varieties to choose from that will thrive as houseplants in small containers. It's not uncommon to find larger varieties that have been grafted, or fused onto the hardy, dwarf tree 'Flying Dragon' (*Poncirus trifoliata*) to keep them small for container culture. 'Key Lime', 'Centennial' kumquat, and 'Meyer' lemon are beautiful choices that don't mind 10–12" pots to begin with.

Good Growing

The key to successfully growing citrus indoors hinges on three things: bright light, consistent moisture, and good drainage. Most of us know that citrus trees thrive in sunny and warm places in the world. In an apartment, this translates to a warm and bright spot such as a south-facing window or underneath a grow light setup that can provide 6 hours of direct sunlight, even in the winter months. Anything less and you're bound to encounter sickness and at the very least a lack of fruit production.

Water plants deeply but infrequently. Always check that the soil has dried slightly, at least a few inches down into the pot, before watering again. Give your plants a monthly shower in the dead of winter if the air is particularly dry in your home.

Airflow and drainage are critical; on the one hand, citrus trees love lots of water, but they will drop leaves and eventually die if that water puddles and stagnates too long. Let the soil dry out slightly before watering again.

Citrus trees are good producers, but making flowers and fruit is hard work. They need lots of nitrogen and appreciate a springtime application of compost, manure, or bloodmeal.

Move your plants outside for the summer and bring them back inside before the first frost. You can grow citrus outdoors year-round in warm climates (above 55°F) too.

Planting

Buy small plants and don't bother with seeds. It can take a decade to grow a seedling to the fruiting stage, and there is no guarantee that what comes out at the end will be like the original plant.

Plant trees in containers that are at least a few inches wider than the root ball but not much deeper. Use potting soil that is nutrient rich, very well draining, and slightly acidic. Although I have never seen specially prepared citrus soil in stores, you can easily improve on a bag of regular potting soil by mixing in 1 part orchid bark or coconut husk chips to 3 parts soil. The bark or chips will increase drainage and acidity.

You'll probably need to replace depleted soil or upgrade to a larger pot in a few years. Simply repeat with fresh soil and a slightly wider pot if the plant is busting out of its current home.

Developing fruit of the 'Centennial' ▶ kumquat are also variegated; citrus flowers will sweetly scent your home.

Currants and Gooseberries

Currants and gooseberries are among the few fruits that cold-climate dwellers get to claim as our own, yet they are almost completely ignored except by the in-the-know few.

Good Growing

Currant and gooseberry bushes won't survive in warm climates. They grow best in full sun where the soil is rich, moist, and well draining with lots of organic matter worked in. Don't skip out on a yearly application of compost; these bushes need a lot of nutrition. They are most susceptible to mildew; see page 73 for details. Birds love them too, but netting will keep them off.

Plant 2-year-old bushes in the early fall, spacing them several feet away from other bushes. Buying an older bush may seem pricey, but don't forget to factor in the decades of service you'll get from one plant!

Black Currant

(*Ribes nigrum*) — Gooseberry Family (Grossulariaceae)

Sweeter and less acidic than the others, black currants are my favorite in this family. I like them best made into jam or juice, but they are most famously known as the basis for a liqueur called cassis.

Black currant bushes produce stems from below the ground. When they are planted in the garden, they need to be dug in 2" deeper than in the pot. Grow a mildew-resistant variety like 'Ben More'. Fruit develops from stems that are a year old. In the fall, prune back branches that have fruited or are weak, all the way to the ground.

The fruit is ready to harvest around mid- to late summer.

GROWING IN POTS

Mulch pots to help retain moisture. In freezing climates, grow in 16" pots and overwinter in a shed or sheltered spot with burlap wrapped around.

Black Currant:
Suitability (Yield): Low
Minimum Depth: 12"
Varieties: 'Ben Sarek'

Gooseberry:
Suitability (Yield): Medium-low
Minimum Depth: 12"
Varieties: 'Pixwell'

Red Currant and White Currant:
Suitability (Yield): Low
Minimum Depth: 12"
Varieties: 'Red Lake', 'White Imperial'

Gooseberry

(*Ribes uva-crispa*) — Gooseberry Family (Grossulariaceae)

Gooseberries produce odd, translucent fruit in a range of colors and textures. They prefer the same conditions as currants but are more tolerant of shade and less tolerant of hot, dry spots. Oddly enough, drought encourages mildew problems. Keep your plants well watered, paying extra attention when the fruit begins to set. They don't need as much nitrogen as other currants, but still like lots of potassium. They also appreciate a little magnesium from Epsom salts.

Get a leg up on disease by growing mildew-resistant varieties such as 'Invicta' or 'Pax'. Gooseberries produce fruit on branches that are 1, 2, and 3 years old. Prune your bushes back in the fall or early spring, removing stems that are unhealthy or older than 3 years. Prune out a few excess branches to reduce mildew when the plants get too thick in the middle. Cut back as far as a young shoot; don't go to the ground as you would with black currant.

Gooseberries are best for jams and pies when harvested just before they ripen in midsummer.

Red Currant and White Currant

(*Ribes sativum*) — Gooseberry Family (Grossulariaceae)

Red and white currants are exactly the same. Red currants prefer a lighter soil than black currants. Aphids and leaf spot are the most common problems but can be controlled with smart companion planting (try chives) and careful pruning to encourage good airflow around the leaves.

Like gooseberries, red and white currants fruit on 1- to 3-year-old branches. Prune the stems back in the same way as gooseberries, either in the fall or just after fruiting ends. The fruit is ready to harvest around midsummer once full color has developed and the fruit is soft to the touch.

Top down: Cut entire clusters of black currants when ripe to ▶ save pruning time later; gooseberry bushes are great small-space producers; red currants grow gobs of fuss-free fruits.

Melons

(Cucumis melo) — Cucurbit Family (Cucurbitaceae)

I can't blame small-space gardeners for skipping melons. They're rambling plants that will make their way around the neighborhood if you let them. I've found them growing in some pretty unconventional spots. A wayward seed won't have trouble growing out of a garbage pile or patch of forgotten soil. I've even seen a watermelon plant taking over a front lawn!

Good Growing

All melons are sun- and heat-loving plants. They need a long, warm growing season to grow flavorful fruit, sometimes as much as 4 months, making it hard to pull off the finicky varieties in cooler climates. Even reasonably good climates can turn against you, with the right conditions one year followed by a cold and wet season the next. Whether it will be a good or bad melon season can be a bit of a crapshoot.

Melons can be a bit demanding about water. They need consistent moisture through most of the growing season, especially from the time of transplant to fruiting. Watering too much while the fruit is developing can also make flavorless melons, so it's important to cut back during the ripening stage and then cut out watering altogether right at harvest time. The crops are drought sensitive during the rest of the season.

And as you can probably guess, making big, juicy fruit takes a lot of energy. Melons like really good, nutrient-rich, well-draining soil. Add compost, manure, sea kelp, and/or bonemeal to the soil at planting time. They like nitrogen early in the season, but cut back once fruit appears.

Melons are susceptible to all the same pests and diseases as their cucurbit cousins. Avoid watering the leaves, cut out some leaves when things get too dense, or train small-fruit varieties up a trellis, where they will get better air circulation. Grow a wilt-resistant variety such as 'Crimson Sweet Watermelon'. Look for squash vine borer at the base of the vine near the soil line and watch out for cucumber beetles, which spread disease in addition to doing damage themselves.

GROWING IN POTS

Use good, nutrient-rich, well-draining soil and keep watered. Grow in a self-watering container, as described in "Set It and Forget It (Well, Almost)" (page 54).

Melon:
Suitability (Yield): Low
Minimum Depth: 12–14"
Varieties: 'Emerald Gem', 'Tigger', 'Jenny Lind', 'Hearts of Gold'
More Tips: Grow dwarf, short-season varieties that produce small fruit.

Watermelon:
Suitability (Yield): Low
Minimum Depth: 14"
Varieties: 'Petite Yellow', 'Golden Midget', 'Cream of Saskatchewan'
More Tips: Grow small "icebox" varieties.

Protect ripening fruit from pests and rot by elevating them up off the ground on top of cans, pie tins, bricks, and broken pots. They'll ripen faster too!

So many beautiful melon varieties are available that you will never want for choice. If you've got the room, try your hand at 'Prescott Fond Blanc,' an amazingly ugly/beautiful variety that is also a little bit drought tolerant. 'Charentais' is a very "popular French heirloom cantaloupe that receives raves for its delicious, sweet flavor. 'Moon and Stars' watermelon is a popular old Amish variety whose speckled plant and fruit look as beautiful as they taste. 'Mountain Sweet Yellow' has a very high sugar content, making it a very yummy summer treat.

With their long list of demands and rambling ways, melons, especially watermelons, are not exactly ideal for container growing. But it can be done. See "Growing in Pots" for details.

Sowing and Planting

Sow seeds indoors around the last frost date, about 1" deep. Plant the seedlings outdoors 3 or more weeks after the last frost date. Melons prefer not to have their roots disrupted. If you can, direct-sow in warm climates or start indoors in big pots rather than tiny seed-starting cells. As with squash plants, I like to bump up the nutrition content of the soil by making 1-foot-wide mounds of compost on top of the soil. I then space three seedlings evenly on the mound. I cover each plant with a plastic bottle with the bottom cut off to keep them snugly warm.

Melon flowers should attract plenty of pollinators, but the flowers don't stay open long. Hand-pollinate to ensure that the job gets done; see "Summer and Winter Squash" (page 114).

Harvesting

Pinch off lingering flowers and new shoots about a month before the first frost. Most melons are ripe when there is a noticeable color change, often from gray-green to yellow or beige. Smell the ends of the fruit; ripe fruit often emits a fragrant aroma. Ripe fruit should still be firm, but stems shrivel and can be easily pulled from the vine.

Watermelons are ripe when the underside turns yellow and the tendril nearest to the fruit dries up. Enjoy!

WHAT'S THE DIFFERENCE?

Cantaloupes traditionally have a hard, warty rind, unlike **muskmelons**, which have soft rinds covered in "netting" and a sweet, orange flesh inside. Confusingly, North Americans consider cantaloupes what the rest of the world identifies as muskmelons. **Honeydews** are melons with smooth, yellowish rinds and flesh that can be green, white, yellow, orange, or anything in between. **Watermelons** are large to extra-large smooth-skinned melons that come in a range of colors and are often striped. The interior flesh can range from almost white to yellow, pink, or red.

Strawberries

(*Fragaria*) — Rose Family (Rosaceae)

I used to be partial to the gigantic, juicy hybrid strawberries, boasting when I grew a particularly big one, and always under the mistaken assumption that the biggest berries were best.

And then I tried a wild strawberry. Those tiny, thimble-sized berries may be small, but boy, do they pack a punch. Honestly, any homegrown strawberry is better than the watery, factory-farmed giants. They're all worth growing and easy to do in a space as small as a hanging basket or window box.

Good Growing

Strawberries are closely associated with summer, so it should come as no surprise that they prefer a place in the sun. Still, they don't mind a little bit of shade, and the smaller wild types can even be grown underneath taller plants as a ground cover. They do best in rich, moist, but not waterlogged soil that leans slightly to the acidic side. Add compost at planting time or as a side-dressing (page 65) in the spring, but don't go crazy with the fertilizer or you'll grow a lot of big, bland berries. Mulch with straw in the early spring to lock in moisture and raise the berries up off the ground. Blanket the plants with straw after a hard frost to provide winter protection.

Strawberries are most susceptible to powdery mildew and rot in overcrowded conditions. Keep the runners under control and pull out old plants. A floating row cover or light net draped over the plants before they ripen will keep the birds off. For something different, try growing variegated plants or hybrids such as 'Pink Panda' or 'Lipstick' that have pretty pink flowers.

GROWING IN POTS

Ideal for hanging baskets and window boxes.

Strawberries:
Suitability (Yield): High
Minimum Depth: 6"
Varieties: 'Mara des Bois', 'Brighton'; try alpine varieties in shadier spots.
More Tips: Grow single plants in small pots or several in large containers. Space about 8" apart. In freezing climates, wrap pots in burlap and overwinter in the garage or shed.

Sowing and Planting

Strawberry plants reproduce aggressively in the late summer by growing runners, a type of stem that creeps along the soil making new plants wherever it roots. Plant new crops in early spring or late summer from transplants or runners collected from friends. Pair plants with borage, dill, onion, lettuce, coriander, thyme, and fennel; however, keep them clear of the cabbage family. In the ground, give plants ample space, about 18–20" apart, taking care to position the crowns (where the leaves meet the roots) just above the soil line. Plants that are planted too high will dry out, and those that are planted too deep will rot. Remove the blooms in the first year. You'll get a bigger crop in the second year if you can stand to do it.

All strawberries are perennial plants that deserve a permanent spot in the garden; however, hybrid varieties tend to fizzle out after 3 years, producing fewer and smaller berries. Replace the entire bed or phase out old stock with new transplants or runners.

Harvesting

Most strawberries are ripe and ready for picking in early summer, but some keep making new fruit throughout the growing season. See "What's the Difference?" for details. Strawberry leaves are edible too and are most often used as a tea.

WHAT'S THE DIFFERENCE?

Cultivated, hybrid strawberries (*Fragaria × ananassa*) are often grouped according to their flowering and fruiting habits. June-bearing hybrids produce a single, large crop in late spring or early summer, while ever-bearing or perpetual plants produce slightly smaller crops throughout the growing season.

Wild strawberries (*Fragaria vesca*) produce much smaller, but tastier fruit. Cultivated wild plants are known as alpines or *frais des bois*.

CHAPTER 9:

Herbs and Edible Flowers

Herbs and edible flowers make good starter plants for aspiring food gardeners, especially when space is limited. They give the biggest rewards in the shortest amount of time with the least amount of work.

One 15" container of mixed culinary herbs can provide the flavor foundation for a year's worth of meals. The best part is that you can start harvesting within only a few weeks of planting, in some cases continuing to harvest right up to the end of the growing season. You'll likely have enough left over to freeze, dry, and store for the winter's famine.

Understanding Differences

Herbs and edible flowers are often described as fit for a windowsill or small pot, but many of them aren't. Losing one plant after another to this kind of false perception can be frustrating. Not all herbs are small plants, although they appear that way in the store, with every seedling under the sun lined up in rows of matching 4" pots. Before buying, check the tags for the plant's height and girth at maturity.

Next, check for words like *annual*, *perennial*, and *biennial*. These refer to the duration of a plant's life cycle. Annuals live an entire life from seedling to reproduction in one year; perennials last a good 5–10 years, and sometimes even indefinitely. Biennials come somewhere in between, growing leaves in the first year and buying the farm at the end of the second. This rush to live fully in a short period can make annuals a bit more demanding nutrition-wise, while perennials tend to take a more slow and steady approach to life.

Annuals and biennials are best started from seeds and generally do not like to be transplanted. Direct-sowing on the spot is the best way to go. They won't last forever but many will self-seed, returning for a repeat performance year after year. It may seem cheaper to buy seeds, but perennials are best grown from cuttings or transplants because seedlings can sometimes take as long as 3 years to grow big enough to start harvesting.

Other words to look for on tags include *hardy* and *tender*, which indicate a plant's ability to tolerate cold. Most hardy plants can withstand a full-blown winter, but tender plants will perish if temperatures drop too low.

THE BASICS

- Organize your garden around the perennial herbs (and some fruit) since they stay put over the long haul, acting as the structural bones of the garden.

- Most culinary herbs are of Mediterranean origin and prefer lots of sun and well-draining soil.

- Add lots of grit or organic matter to increase drainage in compacted or clay soils.

- If soil isn't on your side, build a raised bed (see page 44).

Herbal Strawberry Pot

Take advantage of the stacked design of strawberry pots (originally meant for growing strawberries) to grow several small herbs within a tight area. Glazed ceramic pots hold water better than unglazed terra-cotta, which tends to dry out quickly. Look for pots with big, deep pockets; many strawberry pots just have slits in the sides, which makes them exceptionally hard to water.

Any of the following combinations will work brilliantly in traditional pots or bins too. Limit a washbasin-sized tub to five or six plants so there's enough room for everyone to spread out a little. Always grow like with like. Plants that prefer sun or shade, dry soil or moist soil, should be grown together.

DESIGN IDEAS AND THEMES

All Mint: Ginger, pear, spearmint, chocolate, banana, peppermint, orange, grapefruit, apple, pineapple.

All Thyme: Great for a small pot. Oregano, lemon, orange spice, rose petal, caraway, silver, variegated lemon.

Herbal Tea: Lavender, lemon balm, mint, chamomile, bee balm, catnip, 'Sacred' basil.

Mediterranean: Sage, rosemary, thyme, oregano, marjoram.

Italian Herb: Sweet basil, Genovese basil, arugula, garlic chives, thyme, marjoram, tarragon.

Dessert Herb: For cakes, ice cream, sorbet. 'Cinnamon' basil, anise basil, caraway, lemon balm, pineapple mint, spearmint, scented geranium (on top), mixed viola and pansy varieties, sacred basil, orange mint.

Salad: Grow in a cooler spot. Red orache, French sorrel, 'Flame' lettuce, 'Red Sails' lettuce, mizuna, 'Mascara' lettuce, 'Wrinkly Crinkly' cress, arugula, chervil.

Edible Flowers: Pansy, viola, nasturtium, chamomile, calendula, mint, dianthus, Gem series marigold, nigella.

Edible Flower Flavor Profiles

CITRUS/ACIDIC

- Tuberous begonia
- 'Lemon' basil
- Lemon verbena
- Lemon and tangerine 'Gem' marigold (*Tagetes tenuifolia*)
- French sorrel (*Rumex acetosa*)

FRESH/FRUITY

- Borage (*Borago officinalis*)
- Spearmint
- Chocolate mint
- Banana mint
- Anise hyssop (*Agastache foeniculum*)
- Dill
- Fennel
- Shiso

SPICY

- Arugula
- Radish
- Chives
- Dianthus (*Dianthus barbatus*)
- Nasturtium
- Nigella (*Nigella sativa*)
- 'Sacred' basil (*Ocimum sanctum*)

FLORAL

- Rose geranium
- Pansy and viola (*Viola* spp.)
- Rose
- Lavender
- Snapdragon
- Bachelor's buttons (*Centaurea cyanus*)

SWEET

- Angelica (*Angelica archangelica*)
- Stevia (*Stevia rebaudiana*)

HERBAL AND AROMATIC

- Bay (*Laurus nobilis*)
- Bronze fennel (*Foeniculum vulgare* 'Purpureum')
- Caraway (*Carum carvi*)
- Catnip (*Nepeta cataria*)
- Hyssop (*Hyssopus officinalis*)
- Calendula (*Calendula officinalis*)
- Chervil (*Anthriscus cerefolium*)
- Salad burnet (*Sanguisorba minor*)
- Oregano
- Wild bergamot (*Monarda* spp.)
- Lovage (*Levisticum officinale*)
- Marjoram (*Origanum majorana*)
- Scented geranium (*Pelargonium*)
- Summer savory (*Satureja hortensis*)
- Tarragon (*Artemisia dracunculus sativa*)
- Vietnamese coriander aka *rau ram* (*Persicaria odorata*)
- Watercress (*Nasturtium officinale*)

Anise Hyssop

(Agastache foeniculum) — Mint Family (Lamiaceae)

PERENNIAL

Anise hyssop first won my heart when it managed to thrive through both a dry, hot summer and a harsh winter in a planter box on my roof. And it has come back every year since . . . and then some. In fact, this beautiful flowering herb can be a bit of a menace. It's an aggressive self-seeder—hours of my life have been lost to picking its progeny from every pot and crevice on my roof. And yet I continue to love it dearly. The taste of this interesting herb is somewhere between mint, fruit, and licorice. The flowers are especially delicious and beautiful too, attracting all sorts of interesting pollinators and butterflies to my garden high up in the sky.

Good Growing

Anise hyssop is a really tolerant plant. It sometimes needs a little attention when it begins to grow, but once established it doesn't mind poor soil, extreme heat, or drought. It's as hardy as they come, withstanding pretty low temperatures. Anise hyssop will grow in containers but gets big enough that it needs real room in order to hit maximum size.

Harvest the leaves and flowers for tea. They're good both fresh and dried.

▲
Anise hyssop is hardy and will thrive just about anywhere.

Basil

(Ocimum) — Mint Family (Lamiaceae)

TENDER ANNUAL

The name *basil* is derived from the Greek word for "king," a name that seems apt given that it clearly reigns supreme with most cooking gardeners. Don't try to fight it. Basil is just so versatile. Although the sweet pesto version has come to define the group, basil is actually a really wide and varied bunch. I once grew thirteen varieties in a year, and they were all completely different in color, size, shape, and flavor. We didn't even need other herbs; we just changed up the basil to suit each meal. Grow gorgeous 'Dark Opal', 'Purple Ruffles', 'Cinnamon', 'Red Rubin', and 'Siam Queen Thai' to bring some color to the edible garden. 'Mrs. Burns' is the freshest of the lemon varieties, and 'African Blue' and 'Sacred' are worth growing for something really different.

Good Growing

The secret to keeping basil happy is patience. Basil is native to some of the warmest places on earth and thrives when there is good soil fertility and warm soil. Not just sun, but warmth. More than any other, this plant dislikes cold, wet weather. It's easy to grow from seed; just don't start too early. Instead, start seeds indoors later than your other plants and wait to set the transplants out until well after the frost-free date has passed to avoid any nasty, out-of-season surprises.

Once it is outdoors, give basil a sunny spot that also has a bit of shelter from very hot sun. That little bit of protection is easy to find under the canopy of a large tomato plant; hence they make very good companions. All basils will grow in containers the right size for the plant. Choose dwarf varieties with small leaves for shallow pots and window boxes. 'Purple Bush' is the prettiest with a surprisingly strong flavor. 'African Blue' and 'West African' are big plants that need big pots, but a better choice on hot and dry fire escapes.

Expand your collection in midsummer by rooting cuttings from developing plants (see page 31).

From top: Tall and space-saving 'Columnar' basil; sweet and spicy 'Sacred' basil. ▶

'Dark Opal' Basil Jelly

This recipe is fantastic made with any of the fruity basil varieties, including 'Cinnamon', 'Anise', 'Lime', and 'Lemon'. 'Cinnamon' basil makes a dead ringer for candied cinnamon spread, and 'Lemon' basil is both tart and fresh. Yum.

If you don't have grape juice, you can substitute pomegranate juice or water. Or, for a sweeter jelly, swap out some of the water for more juice.

This recipe uses low-methoxyl pectin, a type that allows jam and jelly makers to cut back on the sugar (see page 190). As a result, this recipe will not work with regular pectin.

- 1½ cups fresh 'Dark Opal' basil leaves, finely chopped
- ½ cup white grape juice
- ½ cup lemon juice
- 2 cups sugar
- 3 teaspoons low-methoxyl pectin
- 3 teaspoons calcium phosphate solution

If you'd rather not bother with sterilizing jars, leave the jelly on the counter to cool and set for a few hours before serving. It will last about a month in the fridge.

1. Place the basil, white grape juice, and 1½ cups water in a pan and bring it to a boil. Immediately remove the pan from the heat and set aside to steep for about 20 minutes.

2. Strain the leaves from the liquid. Some liquid will have evaporated, so add more water to bring the quantity up to 2 cups.

3. Pour the liquid back into the pan along with the lemon juice and slowly bring the mixture to a boil. In the meantime, mix the sugar and low-methoxyl pectin in a bowl.

4. Once the herbal liquid is boiling, slowly stir in the sugar-pectin mixture using a whisk, continuing to stir until the powders have dissolved into the liquid and all lumps are gone.

5. Bring the liquid to a vigorous rolling boil that can't be stirred down and allow it to boil for 1 minute, stirring constantly.

6. Quickly and thoroughly stir in the calcium phosphate solution and remove the jelly from the heat.

7. Pour into sterilized jars and process in a boiling-water bath (see page 192) for 5 minutes.

Makes 5–6 quarter-pint jars

Bee Balm
aka Wild Bergamot

(Monarda spp.) — Mint Family (Lamiaceae)

PERENNIAL

Bee balm is worth growing for the flowers alone; their feathery plumes attract an assortment of beneficial insects to the garden. Bee balm is known primarily as a tea herb. The flowers, which come in a range of colors from red to pink to lavender, have a flavor that is minty but also deeply aromatic. The leaves are edible too but are stronger and better suited to flavoring heavy meats.

Good Growing

Bee balm is in the mint family, making it an assertive spreader. It prefers soil that is fertile and well draining in a sunny, warm spot. Warmth is the key—it just doesn't like cool soil. The plant is notoriously prone to powdery mildew. Prune to provide good air circulation, especially once the humidity rises in the summer.

Bee balm grows best from cuttings and transplants. You can also divide the roots in the fall to give away to gardening friends.

Borage

(Borago officinalis) — Borage Family (Boraginaceae)

ANNUAL

Borage is an undervalued plant that doesn't seem to register on a lot of gardeners' radar. I don't blame them. The prickly leaves are a real put-off. I ignored the plant entirely until I inherited a community garden plot that was overrun with it. I really came to love its pretty little star-shaped blue flowers. I'll never get over how much the blossoms taste like cucumbers! The young leaves aren't too shabby steamed, but I prefer them tossed into batter for fritters.

Good Growing

Here's a plant that actually prefers poor soil. Fertile soil only encourages borage to grow exceptionally tall and lanky. The plants in my garden need stakes! For that reason it is one of the few herbs considered inappropriate for containers. Toss some seeds in a sunny spot and you'll have plants seeding themselves in the garden for years to come. Borage is said to improve the flavor of tomatoes. I don't know if this is true, but I always grow some nearby just in case.

Calendula
aka Pot Marigold

(*Calendula officinalis*) — Aster/Composite Family (Asteraceae)

ANNUAL

Calendula is a must-have flower in the edible garden. Once it starts blossoming it will produce endless, cheerful blooms, especially in moderate climates where it can continue through the winter. All parts of the plant are edible, but I like the petals best as a natural food dye in rice and baked goods. Calendula attracts a wide assortment of beneficial insects and is considered a very good companion to crops in the cabbage family and a deterrent to tomato hornworm.

Good Growing

Calendula thrives in rich, well-draining soil where there is lots of light. It's prone to fungal problems in damp, airless conditions, so try to be aggressive about pulling out the extras that will inevitably germinate all on their own, year after year. Direct-sow by lightly tossing the seeds across the soil in early spring. You'll never need to do this again.

Calendula is prized among herbalists as a potent skin salve ingredient. The common yellow and orange varieties are so strong they practically drip oils. Many other less potent and prettier varieties are available for curiosity seekers. Try 'Antares Flashback' and 'Triangle Flashback', both of which have subtle apricot petals that are light on top and dark maroon underneath. 'Radio' is an old favorite with spiky, quilled petals.

From top: Colorful 'Triangle Flashback' calendula: dried for storage (top) and fresh (bottom). ▶

Chamomile
aka Roman Chamomile

(Chamaemelum nobile) — Aster/Composite Family (Asteraceae)

PERENNIAL

Roman chamomile is a low-growing spreader that is most prized as a popular herbal chill-out tea. Chamomile pretty much grows itself, and I recommend adding it to your garden even if you're allergic like me. It's a good companion, offering strength to ailing neighbors and attracting loads of parasitic wasps and hoverflies to take out problem bugs. Serve it up to young seedlings as an antifungal remedy that can help prevent damping-off disease (page 73).

Good Growing

Roman chamomile is a hardy plant that does best in a sunny spot but will stay alive pretty much anywhere you put it. Its only gripe is with wet soil, so make sure yours drains well or plant the chamomile in a pot instead. Sow the tiny seeds indoors or out in the spring.

Snip blooms off after they have opened and lay them flat to dry, or keep some stem and hang if space is an issue.

Cilantro
aka Coriander

(Coriandrum sativum) — Carrot Family (Apiaceae)

ANNUAL

Cilantro is a divisive plant. People either love it or insist it tastes like soap. I sit firmly on the "love it" side. Salsa just isn't right without freshly chopped cilantro.

Good Growing

Like most herbs, cilantro prefers to grow in full sun with well-draining soil. It's not too picky about soil fertility and does well in pots of all sizes. The only real trouble is that it is quick to bolt as soon as the summer heat picks up. Start clipping back the flowers (and eat those tasty morsels), and when you can't fight it any more, let the plant go to seed. You can eat them too! They have a lemony citrus flavor that is quite unlike the leaves. It's a two-for-one deal in the same plant!

Direct-sow seed in early spring. Don't bother with transplants; they just bolt faster.

Dill

(Anethum graveolens) — Carrot Family (Apiaceae)

ANNUAL

I always seem to grow way more dill than I can possibly eat, lured to let the zillions of bonus plants that pop up all over the place grow because they promise future tall and statuesque flowers. Those beautiful umbrellas attract all kinds of parasitic wasps and pollinators, making dill a helpful plant despite its pushy, self-seeding ways.

Good Growing

Direct-sow dill in early spring (if you dare). It doesn't like to be moved and germinates so readily that transplants are a waste of money. Grow in a really sunny spot that has well-draining soil with decent nutrition. Dill isn't too picky. It's a delicate yet resilient plant that will adapt to poor situations by staying small. Harvest the leaves as you need them and let some plants produce mature seeds that you can harvest just in time for pickle season. Keep dill away from fennel; they'll cross-pollinate.

Blooming Ice Cubes

Prim and proper Victorian women added borage blossoms to their drinks and salads as a lunching ladies' "mood lifter." Gussy up your average chilly beverage by embedding the flowers in water. Simply grab the petal portion of an edible flower, such as borage, mint, lavender, or rose geranium, and yank it free from its base. Place a single blossom in each chamber of an ice cube tray. Fill with cold water, freeze, and serve in a tall glass of water with a thin cucumber slice added for flavor.

Lavender

(Lavandula) — Mint Family (Lamiaceae)

PERENNIAL

Lavender is more often praised for its invigorating scent in health and beauty products than for its culinary usefulness. Relaxing teas are the most popular use, but a little creativity can give you a wonderful result in baked goods and meaty dishes.

Good Growing

All lavender, even the hardier English varieties, can be fickle about the weather. I've had plants last for years until a harsh winter took them down. In northern climates, choose hardier, dwarf varieties like 'Munstead' and 'Hidcote'. Moderate-climate gardeners have their pick, with loads of fascinating, tender French varieties to choose from.

Lavender is another Mediterranean herb that likes lots of sun and tolerates drought well. The soil is critical and must be well draining; lavender hates humidity and dampness. All lavender types grow well in containers, but it is important to know the variety because some can grow to be big, woody bushes.

Grow lavender from transplants and cuttings because seeds just take too darn long. Use the leaves whenever you need them and harvest the flower in summer, just before the buds open.

Lemon Balm

(Melissa officinalis) — Mint Family (Lamiaceae)

PERENNIAL

Lemon balm is a tasty herb with a mild, lemony flavor that is best brewed fresh or dried as a stomach-soothing herbal tea, mixed into salad dressing, or served as a garnish with fruit. To say that this plant is prolific would be an understatement. I've affectionately dubbed it "the lemon bomb" because one plant introduced to a garden will explode the following spring, sprouting zillions of tiny seedlings far and wide.

Good Growing

Despite its opportunistic ways, lemon balm is a blessing for shady gardeners; it's one of the few edibles that don't seem to mind that gloomy spot underneath the maple tree. One of the first herbs up in the earliest spring, lemon balm provides a harvest before most other perennials have woken up from their winter slumber. It grows best in a cool spot with rich, moist soil, but even lousy dirt doesn't seem to stop it in my garden. Lemon balm tends to crowd itself out. Pull some out and prune large plants back to maintain good air circulation and stave off rust and other fungal problems.

Lemon balm grows easily from directly sown seeds or transplants set out in early spring. Don't bother buying it; someone you know is bound to have a few thousand extras to spare.

The best harvest comes before flowers appear in early summer. If you prune the plants way back at harvest time and keep them pruned before seeds come, you just may be able to hold them back from multiplying like a maniac.

Herbal Iced Tea

These unusual riffs on the classic iced tea concept will give you a new way to use up and enjoy the herbs in your garden.

1. Boil a pot of water and then set the pot or kettle aside for a couple of minutes to cool down slightly. Steeping the leaves in boiled water ruins the integrity of the herb's essential oils.

2. Place lightly chopped fresh herbs into a teapot and pour hot water over the top. Starting out with a strong brew will prevent the inevitable flavor flop that comes from using lots of ice cubes. Use 1 tablespoon of fresh herbs per cup of water to keep the tea flavor amped. When using dried herbs, reduce the quantity by half.

3. Steep to taste. Each herb is different and can take anywhere between 5 and 15 minutes to hit its peak.

4. Stir in sweetener to taste to dissolve while the tea is still warm.

5. Set in the fridge to cool.

6. Add lots of ice cubes and serve.

Dip the moistened rim of each glass into a shallow plate of Herb-Infused Sugar (page 161) and add a little extra flair to your drink.

Lemon Ginger Zinger

A zingy, tangy tea with enough pep to give you a caffeine-free jolt.

- 2 parts lemon verbena
- 1 part lemon balm
- 1 part ginger mint
- ½ part grated fresh ginger
- Sweetener

Citrus Buzz

This caffeine-free brew is both aromatic and uplifting with a hint of mint and citrus fruit. The herbal combination will also work wonders on an upset stomach.

- 1 part bee balm (*Monarda didyma*)
- 1 part orange mint
- 1 part lemon basil
- Sweetener

Zesty Refresh

This blend is both spicy and unexpectedly refreshing. We put this one to the test on a painfully hot summer day, and it was downed in one gulp.

- 1 part 'Cinnamon' basil
- 1 part lemon balm
- Orange zest
- Orange slice to garnish
- Sweetener

Fuzzy Peach

Using frozen peaches makes a drink that is frothy, yet not as thick as a smoothie. Lavender brings out surprising subtle floral notes in the peaches and actually makes the fruit taste sweeter.

- 1 tablespoon lavender blossoms
- 1 teaspoon honey, or to taste
- 3 frozen peaches, sliced

1. Brew a cup of lavender tea according to the preceding directions. Sweeten with honey to taste.

2. Place the sweetened tea and frozen peach slices in a blender. Blend until smooth.

3. Add lots of ice cubes and serve.

MIX IT UP

Try your hand at mixing up your own blends and concoctions.

Refreshing: Mint, anise hyssop, basil, and shiso

Spicy: 'Cinnamon' basil, ginger, and cinnamon

Floral: Rose petals, rose hips, rose geranium, lavender, jasmine, hibiscus, and 'Sacred' basil

Fruity: Lemon verbena, lemon balm, 'Lemon' basil, chamomile, lemon thyme, pineapple sage, citrus zest (peel), apple geranium, and raspberry leaf

Unusual: Sage, hyssop, rosemary, and thyme

Lemon Verbena

(Aloysia triphyllum) — Verbena Family (Verbenaceae)

TENDER PERENNIAL

There's only one way to describe lemon verbena: best lemon-flavored herb bar none. It's just so bright, fresh, and crisp, even after it's been dried and sitting in the cupboard for months. The leaves are best used in teas, desserts, and jelly; the lemon-sucker sweetness is too intense for main dishes.

Good Growing

Grow lemon verbena in a 12" pot. The transplants look small in the store but will grow into a big, woody shrub in no time. This is no window box herb! Grow it in soil that has very good drainage and set it in the sun or against a warm wall. Water it well. It doesn't mind a little drought but gets tough and burned-looking if the soil stays dry too long. Lemon verbena flowers late in the season. Let it go and enjoy! The flowers are as powerfully sweet and aromatic as the leaves.

Grow lemon verbena from cuttings or transplants. One plant is plenty. Warm-climate gardeners can keep theirs outdoors year-round, but the plant will have to be brought in wherever the temperature dips below 40°F. Keep yours near a window in a cool, out-of-the-way spot and water occasionally to keep it from drying out. As a deciduous plant it will drop all of its leaves for the winter—a bare bush in the window may not fit into your living room's décor. Put it back outside in late spring when all threat of frost has passed.

Mint

(Mentha spp.) — Mint Family (Lamiaceae)

PERENNIAL

How else to describe mint but greedy? Give this plant its own special place in the garden and it will push out its neighbors soon enough. Gardeners try to rein it in by planting barriers, but this plant has a strong will. It always finds a way. And yet I don't mind a bit because mint is good stuff. And there are so many flavors to try! My love affair with 'Chocolate Mint' is undying, but there's also proper Cuban 'Mojito' to consider—much warmer than regular mint in the popular drink. Don't forget 'Orange', 'Grapefruit', and the prettiest of them all: 'Ginger'. Give them all their own space so they can maintain their potency.

Good Growing

Mint prefers rich, moist soil with good drainage to keep rust at bay, and some sun, but is perfectly okay with a bit of shade.

Don't bother with seeds or buying transplants. Just nick a cutting from a friend and you're set for life.

Clockwise from top: 'Empress of India' ▶ nasturtium growing on a window ledge; oregano blossoms are pretty and edible, too; even the smallest garden will produce armfuls of fresh mint.

Nasturtium

(*Tropaeolum majus*) — Nasturtium Family (Tropaeolaceae)

ANNUAL

Nasturtiums, or "nasties" for short, are the supreme rulers of the edible flower world, producing charming, round leaves and large flowers that are at once peppery and sweet. I can only imagine that the nickname comes from the West Coast, where the climate causes these plants to grow bigger and badder than anything I've seen in the northeast. Nasturtium plants vary between mounding, vining, sprawling, and climbing depending on the variety. But on the West Coast they're all King Kong sized!

Good Growing

Nasturtiums make an excellent ground cover under taller plants. Unfortunately, they're also an aphid magnet, sometimes hosting dozens of aphids on one flower bud. Shudder. Their tenacious nature really depends on growing conditions. They grow best in rich, moist soil with lots of legroom but will tolerate poor conditions and can even adjust to life in a window box. I prefer the small and pretty 'Empress of India' in mine. They make an impression with deep green leaves and dark red flowers. 'Alaska Mix' is a popular variegated variety whose flowers pop up in a crayon box of colors. If you're looking for something to climb up a trellis, choose vibrant and lush 'Spitfire'.

Direct-sow nasturtium seeds after the danger of frost has passed. Start plucking the flowers once they appear, and they'll keep making more until a hard frost wipes them out. Let some plants produce seeds—they're really good pickled.

Oregano & Marjoram

(*Origanum vulgare*) and (*Origanum majorana*) — Mint Family (Lamiaceae)

PERENNIAL

Oregano is a highly aromatic yet versatile cooking herb that is not to be missed in an edible garden, if you can manage to find aromatic stock in your local garden shop. Most of the plants I find these days have diluted, flavorless leaves that lack that characteristic Mediterranean punch. For this reason, I've switched my allegiance to its less hardy, perfumy cousin marjoram. I use a pinch in stocks, soups, and sauces with the same enthusiasm I once held for oregano.

Good Growing

Both plants do best in full sun with well-draining soil; however, I've had luck with oregano in shadier spots too. The plant is pretty aggressive and has gone head to head with mint and won. Both plants are drought tolerant and grow easily in containers and window boxes of all sizes. If you can't resist having it fresh during the winter, you're in luck; either plant can bear a few months on a sunny windowsill. Keep pruning if the plant starts to grow lanky.

Grow oregano and marjoram from transplants or divisions taken from friends. Seeds germinate easily, but the flavor can't be guaranteed. Let your plants flower and they'll attract an assortment of beneficial insects. Golden leaf varieties, including the spirally 'Aureum Crispum', create a nice contrast set next to purple plants or blue lobelia.

Clockwise from top left: 'Purple' sage is semihardy in cold climates; brew rosemary into a cup of soothing stress-relief tea; flat-leaved parsley; 'Purple' shiso will self-seed in the garden for years to come. ▶

Parsley

(Petroselinum spp.) — Carrot Family (Apiaceae)

BIENNIAL

Parsley is a kitchen staple that tastes good in everything. It was the first plant I ever grew as a kid, but it fell out of favor in my adult years. I've recently brought it back but prefer the less popular flat-leaved variety. I'm in the minority because the curly type is more ornamental, favored as a garnish, easier to grow, and less apt to bolt in the heat.

Good Growing

Parsley grows best in the sun but doesn't mind a shadier spot. It likes rich, moist, well-draining soil but really isn't fussy. Even a five-year-old can grow it. I did! Only the slugs seem to bother it, but not enough to worry about.

Parsley seeds are notoriously difficult to germinate. Give the hard shell a helping hand with a few light scratches across a piece of sandpaper. Or easier yet, skip the seeds and buy a plant. Even one plant is enough to keep you in fresh and dried leaves for a season or two. Let it go to seed in the second season and the crop will self-perpetuate into infinity.

Rosemary

(Rosmarinus officinalis) — Mint Family (Lamiaceae)

TENDER PERENNIAL

I dream of having a garden surrounded by aromatic rosemary hedges. Alas, a northern climate is not the place to make that happen. Rosemary is a tough plant, but it can't bear temperatures that fall below 15°F and must be brought inside in cold climates. If the weather is on your side, don't be limited to the classic upright variety; some trailing types can be put to remarkable use in edible landscapes.

Good Growing

Rosemary is a seaside plant with a Mediterranean heritage. As a result it does best in full sun with slightly sandy, well-draining soil. Rosemary can reach the size of a large and sprawling shrub, but is slow growing and adapts well to pots of all sizes.

Don't bother with seeds; they take too long, while cuttings will root in no time at all. Rosemary is not an easy plant to overwinter indoors and is prone to drying out. The trick is to wait until it's been nipped by a light frost before bringing it inside. Keep it somewhere moderately cool like an unheated garage and give it a weekly spritz from the spray bottle to mimic the ocean's spray. Snip off top bits and pieces when you need it for cooking. Rosemary is a classic with roasted potatoes and soups and also makes a very good headache-healing tea.

Herb-Infused Salt or Sugar

Making my own mix of herbs and salt or sugar seemed like a wasted effort better spent reading a book or, say, clipping my toenails, until I actually did it. Now it's my go-to seasoning for every dish!

Herbed salts are really good on tomatoes, eggs, potatoes, and roasted veggies or rubbed onto fish and meat. Make fruity herbal sugar to dust on the rim of a beverage glass, sweeten iced tea, or sprinkle on top of baked goods. You can also use this recipe to make spicy hot-pepper salt—just a pinch complements chocolate desserts.

Dried herbs can be substituted for fresh but won't lend the same flavor to the salt or sugar and should spend far less time in the oven.

1. Work some of the herb oils into the salt or sugar by lightly pounding them together in a mortar and pestle.

2. Spread the mixture onto a cookie sheet or baking dish and heat slowly in the oven on the lowest possible temperature until the herbs are dried. This can take anywhere from 15 minutes to 1 hour, depending on the herb and your oven's lowest temperature.

3. Set aside to cool and pour the ingredients into a glass jar to store.

Makes about 1 cup

- 1 cup (fine or coarsely ground) sea salt or evaporated cane juice sugar
- 1 cup fresh herb leaves only, finely chopped

Herbs for Salt: Basil, chives, lavender, marjoram, oregano, rosemary, tarragon, and thyme

Herbs for Sugar: Anise hyssop, lavender, mint, 'Cinnamon' basil, lemon basil, anise basil, scented geranium, fruit sage, and bronze fennel

Sage

(Salvia officinalis) — Mint Family (Lamiaceae)

PERENNIAL

There are hundreds of salvias worldwide, but the common hardy garden sage is by far the most popular edible of the bunch. The potent, aromatic leaves are best used where the flavor doesn't overpower the meal; chicken and eggs are popular accompaniments, but I like it most steeped in olive oil and poured on top of a hearty squash soup.

Good Growing

A mature sage plant is a beast of a thing that will grow into a large, woody bush if you let it. Sage thrives most successfully when allowed to spread out in a big pot, but won't stress out too much in a smaller one and adapts really well to containers. Garden sage is rugged and tough, withstanding wind, drought, and hot sun. On the other hand, it is prone to powdery mildew. Make sure to give it a sunny spot with good drainage and clear off any debris or excess leaves to increase airflow.

Prune out dead and broken bits in the spring or cut back if you don't want flowers. I can't imagine why you wouldn't, though. The flowers make an already ornamental plant even prettier, and they're edible too! Grow the classic blue-gray variety or splash out with less hardy colorful varieties such as 'Purple', 'Tricolor', and 'Golden'. 'Berggarten' is a gray plant with charming round leaves.

Sage can be slow-growing from seed. One transplant is cost-effective—the thing will be huge within the year!

Shiso

(Perilla frutescens) — Mint Family (Lamiaceae)

ANNUAL

Shiso is an aggressive self-seeder but worth growing for its unbelievably gorgeous, ruffled foliage. The common variety is green, but it also comes in a purple-red variety that glows when the sunlight shines through the leaves. Stunning flower spikes emerge in the late summer.

The flavor of shiso is hard to place, but I'd describe it as having a bright, fruity citrus essence with a hint of mint. The green variety tends to be less fruity with spicier notes. Shiso is best known as an herbal leaf wrap for rice and sashimi, but I prefer to turn my homegrown stash into an icy and refreshing summer beverage (see "Super Shiso Slush," opposite page).

Good Growing

Shiso is easy to grow from seed. Just toss a few on the soil in late spring. It grows biggest and best in a sunny spot with fertile, well-draining soil and good moisture but doesn't seem to mind a bit of shade. 'Britton', an ornamental variety with green leaves and rusty-maroon undersides, seems to fare a bit better in drier, sunnier spots and smaller pots. Shiso grows well in medium-sized pots, but don't underestimate its size; one plant can grow to be 4' tall and several inches wide.

Super Shiso Slush

Keep a bunch of this mix in the freezer to cool off a hot summer afternoon. To make the best-tasting slush, use the ruffle-leafed purple variety. It turns out a gorgeous bright crimson-colored liquid. You can always add in a bit of green shiso if you're low on purple.

Alternatively, transform your pitcher into an instant "party" beverage with the addition of a couple of ounces of cold sake, *cachaça* (sugarcane liquor), or white rum.

- 1 cup purple shiso leaves
- 2 tablespoons orange juice, optional
- 2 tablespoons honey, or to taste

1. Steep the shiso leaves in 3 cups hot, but not quite boiling, water for 5–10 minutes.

2. Strain the brew into a freezer-proof container with a watertight lid. Recycled yogurt and margarine containers work like a charm.

3. Add the orange juice, if using, and honey to taste while the liquid is still warm, and stir in well.

4. Allow the mix to come to room temperature on the counter, then pop the container into the freezer and forget about it. It should take a good 6–10 hours to freeze, but you can always pull it out early at the "slush" stage and skip ahead to step 6.

5. Remove from the freezer 20–30 minutes before use and set on the counter to thaw slightly. Break the block up into smaller chunks with a large spoon or fork and blend on your blender's "ice crush" setting until smooth.

6. Serve in a glass topped with a skewer of fruit and a sprig of fresh shiso to garnish.

Serves 2

Sunflower

(Helianthus annuus) — Aster/Composite Family (Asteraceae)

ANNUAL

Sunflowers are the cheeriest plant in the garden, grown for their massive flowers and towering presence—some varieties can grow to be 14' tall! The petals are a lesser-known edible part, but even less appreciated still are the immature flower buds, which can be steamed and eaten like artichokes if you can bear to cut them off early.

Good Growing

As the name implies, sunflowers need ample sunlight to grow big and strong, at least 6 hours a day of direct sun. Big plants need lots of water but despite their size are surprisingly problem-free. That may be because they're almost like an ecosystem unto themselves; their flowers attract all kinds of beneficial insects.

Sunflower blooms naturally face east; locate them accordingly in your garden or you'll be stuck looking at the backs. Grow the giants in garbage cans or self-watering containers (see "Set It and Forget It [Well, Almost]," page 54). Dwarf varieties don't mind smaller, foot-deep pots. Try compact seed producers such as 'Sunspot' or 'Big Smile'. Of the giants, try 'Arikara', 'Mongolian Giant', or 'Mammoth Gray Striped'. All sorts of colorful sunflowers exist too, although most won't grow seeds. 'Double Dandy' is a compact plant with lush, red blooms.

◀ Clockwise from top left: 'Silver' and 'Lemon' thymes pair beautifully; 'Strawberry Blonde' sunflower; wrap soon-to-be-harvested sunflower heads with plastic mesh or fabric to keep birds off the goods; 'Chocolate Cherry' sunflower.

Sunflower seedlings don't like to be transplanted. Direct-sow them outdoors after danger of frost has passed or start them indoors 2 weeks before the last frost in toilet paper rolls (see "Toilet Roll Seed-Starting Cells," page 27).

Cover seed heads with mesh or open-weave fabric just after they start to mature if you want some for yourself by harvest time. Behead the stalk just after it turns brown and has lost most of its petals. Cure the heads in a warm, dry spot until the hulls are hard.

Thyme

(Thymus spp.) — Mint Family (Lamiaceae)

PERENNIAL

For such a small plant, thyme takes a prominent position in my garden. It's a really easygoing, sprawling herb that can be crammed into crevices and subjected to all manner of neglect. If you can't grow much else, chances are that you can grow thyme. And with so many varieties to choose from, it never gets dull. I've been rocking a contrasting 'Lemon Variegated' and 'Silver' combo in containers for years but am now expanding into fragrant varieties like 'Nutmeg', 'Orange Spice', and 'Rose Petal'.

Good Growing

Thyme is a sun lover, although I've had lots of luck in shadier spots. It makes a very unobtrusive yet stunning ground cover underneath all sorts of taller edibles and even other herbs. Let it flower and it will bring pollinating insects to the plants that need them. Start plants from cuttings or transplants. Don't bother with the hassle of growing from seed unless you're planning to cover a large space.

Reaping the Harvest

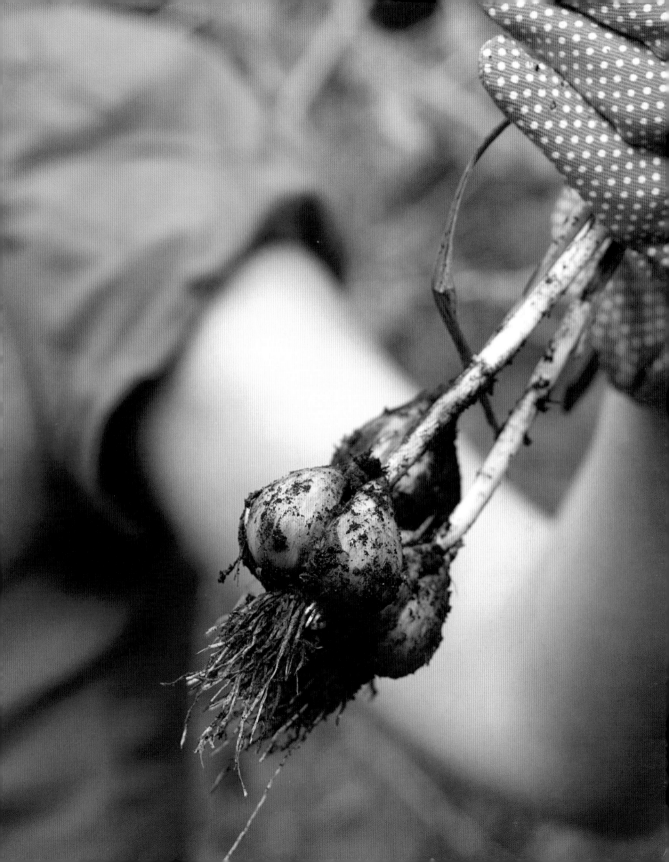

CHAPTER 10:

How to Harvest

Knowing exactly when and how to collect goodies from the garden can be a little intimidating. Luckily even new gardeners have a lifetime of eating experience under their belt as a gauge to follow when choosing a ripe zucchini or eggplant.

The whole process comes down to just some basic birds and bees with a splash of trial and error thrown in. Let's reach back into recent (or slightly less recent) memory and recall some basic high-school biology. Seed turns to plant, plant makes flowers, flowers develop into fruit, and plant dies. The end. Well, it's not always exactly that way, but I've simplified the equation to best explain the basic life cycle of your average kitchen garden annual. Your goal as a gardener and hopeful eater is to beat the plant at its own game by picking fruit (the seed part) when it is young and tender. Once the plant has produced mature fruit, it gets the notion that its earthly deed is done and will call it quits soon after. Procreation is hard work! No retirement cruises await zucchinis and pumpkins. The key here is in finding that fine line between what qualifies as ripe from an eater's point of view (tasty) versus ripe from the plant's perspective (reproductive) and then beating that plant to the punch. The faster you harvest, the more the plant will produce as it strives to realize its legacy.

Of course, there is a small hitch. Harvest times may vary not only from plant to plant but also between varieties of the same plant. Some are simply faster than others. And some are just plain different. For example, how do you tell when a green tomato variety is ripe? This is where education, practice, and experience come in. When growing a new variety, consult photos online to get an idea of what yours should look like at harvest time. Some variety names offer a key to the desired outcome. Hands off that reddish tomato if the package reads 'Black Krim'.

The Harvest Chart on page 173 provides a good starting point in understanding a given crop's life cycle. Section 2 will guide you through the finer points for harvesting individual crops. Read on for general harvesting tips applicable to all crops within larger categories; this information will help you maximize the quality and quantity of your harvest so that you can reap buckets of the most aromatic herbs, juiciest fruit, and luscious vegetables possible from even the smallest space.

I've equipped you with the basics, but some learning is still going to happen right in the garden through experience. Allow yourself to make mistakes on your first, second, or hundredth time out. You will not be receiving a report card in Harvesting 101. Don't sweat it.

LOOKING FOR RIPE

Look: Examine the spot where the fruit is joined to the plant, looking for a withered stem or dry leaves that separate easily from the fruit. Root vegetables often announce their readiness by pushing their top up above the soil slightly. Potatoes are ready when the entire plant dies back. Get more leaves from herbs by cutting off flower buds as soon as they appear. Ripe eggplants are shiny, not dull.

Touch: Soft fruit like raspberries, blackberries, and tomatoes are at their peak when they practically fall off the plant. Peas are ready when the little pills feel slightly firm inside the pod. Hard little marbles generally indicate overdoneness.

Smell: Get down in the dirt next to a hard-skinned melon and give it a little sniff. Melons emit a strong fruity smell from the blossom end when sweet and ready to eat.

Listen: Lightly tap a watermelon with your finger. It should make a hollow sound when ripe.

Ripening Tomatoes: No matter how well you plan, there are always a few unripe tomatoes that don't make it to maturity before the frost hits. Although a sunny window seems like the natural place to ripen a tomato, it turns out that sunlight is not actually required. Instead, wrap individual tomatoes in a piece of newspaper or a paper bag and place them in a warm spot—the top of the fridge is perfect. Turn the remainders into chutney or relish, or batter up and fry. Tasty!

HARVESTING TIPS AT A GLANCE

Pick More, Get More: Regardless of how and when they get around to it, plants have a singular goal: to reproduce. A plant knows to pack it in as soon as this goal is achieved. Picking beans or zucchinis when they are young and tender tricks the plant into trying again. The same goes for herbs and flowers. Removing the flowers before they turn to seed means more flowers and healthy leaves for you.

Small Is More: It's tempting to try to grow oversized produce—you could feed a whole family with a single monster zucchini. Unfortunately it won't taste very good. Overgrown vegetables are woody, hard, and bland.

Fresh Is Best: Most vegetables are at their peak flavor directly after leaving the plant. The longer your harvest sits around on a counter, the lower the quality. Get the most from your pickings by eating or preserving them right away.

In the Morning: Just about all produce is at its freshest, crispest, and tastiest in the early morning. The cooler late evening makes a reasonable substitute for gathering heat-sensitive vegetables and greens.

Predicting the Harvest

About a million factors, including soil fertility and the weather, can wildly affect the harvest times of any given crop. Something as deceptively simple as a bean belongs to a vastly diverse group, with harvest times ranging between 50 and 100 days from seed to harvest. You'll never be able to pinpoint the exact "date of delivery" for any crop, but using the Harvest Chart below will give you some idea of when to start digging around in the soil. Use it again later in the season to make sure you get that late-summer crop in the soil with enough time before the frost.

More advanced gardeners will find the Harvest Chart helpful as a chronicle of how varieties change from season to season.

HARVEST CHART

- Fill in the date you planted the seeds in the "Date Planted" column.
- Calculate the "Expected Harvest" by adding the "Harvest" (number of days listed) to your "Date Planted."
- Record the "Actual Harvest" date when the first day of harvesting arrives.
- Keep tabs on the bounty by filling in the "Yield" column.

CROP	DATE PLANTED	HARVEST	EXPECTED HARVEST	ACTUAL HARVEST	YIELD
• Beans (shelling)		60–90 days			
• Beans (snap)		50–65 days			
• Beets		50–60 days			
Broccoli		60–100 days			
Cabbage		60–100 days			
• Carrot		50–90 days			
Cauliflower		60–90 days			
Cucumber		50–70 days			
Eggplant		65–100 days			
• Lettuce & Greens		20–65 days			
• Kale		50–65 days			
Melon		70–110 days			
• Onion		100–120 days			
• Peas		50–85 days			
Pepper		60–100 days			
• Potato		65–100 days			
Pumpkin		80–120 days			
• Radish		20–30 days			
• Spinach		45–60 days			
Squash (summer)		35–70 days			
Squash (winter)		70–120 days			
• Swiss Chard		50–60 days			
Tomato		60–90 days			

• Indicates direct-sown seeds

CHAPTER 11

Future Fresh: Storing and Preserving the Good Stuff

Even small container gardens can surprise you with too much too soon. Summer and winter squashes are famous for drowning gardeners in abundance; we've all heard the stories. Herbs have a tendency to kick into high gear and subsequently kick the bucket in the blink of an eye.

Spoiled food gone to waste is one thing, but wasted food that you grew yourself is just depressing.

Knowing how to preserve the food you grow is almost as important as knowing how to grow it. It does take a bit of effort, but it isn't hard at all. In fact, most preserving can be done with a friend and a cheesy movie or favorite album playing in the background. It also happens to be incredibly satisfying work with rewards that keep on giving. Stocking up my paltry apartment cupboards and wheezing freezer gives me a sense of pride, comfort, and deep appreciation. I love knowing that I can always open up a jar of homemade salsa or a bag of frozen raspberries and relive the tastes and colors of summer all over again no matter what it looks like outside.

Growing perennial herbs and onions ▶ means you'll have early and late season harvests to look forward to.

Short-Term Storage

Leafy Greens

Wash the leaves and heads of greens in cool water directly after harvesting. Shake, pat, or spin off excess water and store in the crisper section of the fridge in a moistened dish towel storage bag (page 176).

Vegetables and Fruit

Lots of veggies and some fruit keep well in the crisper section of your fridge. On the low end of the spectrum, berries, okra, beans, zucchini, and radishes last only a couple of days, while cabbage and carrots just seem to keep going and going like the Energizer Bunny, lasting up to a month or even longer, depending on the variety. Keep unripe fruit and vegetables on the counter to ripen, but get them in the fridge as soon as they're ready to eat.

Tomatoes are better kept on the counter because they tend to lose their flavor in the fridge. Potatoes, garlic, onions, pumpkins, and winter squash are all better stored in a cool, dark spot outside the fridge because the cold moist air can encourage decay or even prompt them to start sprouting.

I know you want to be clean and tidy, but don't bother washing veggies until you are ready to use them. They'll last longer this way because abrasions and bruising can occur with even the most delicate baths.

Sew Your Own Dish Towel Storage Bags

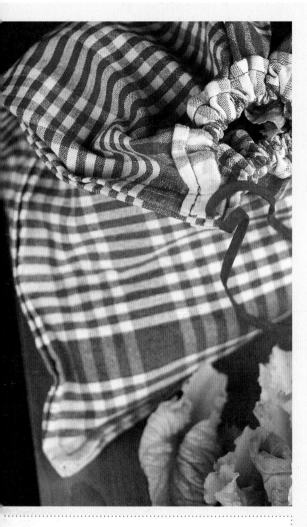

Leafy greens and fresh herbs are notoriously difficult keepers, quickly rotting in plastic bags but wilting into a flaccid pile without some sort of coverage to keep moisture in. A cold, damp cloth provides the best of both worlds, locking in moisture yet allowing the greens to breathe. These simple, easy-sew cloth bags will keep your harvest crisp and rot-free in the fridge.

1. To make the drawstring, lay the dish towel flat, right side facing up and the short side at the top. Position the string about ½" from the right, laying it along the length.

2. Fold the long edge of the towel over the string. Pin in place and stitch a seam straight down, being careful to avoid sewing over the string.

3. Fold the towel in half lengthwise, wrong sides facing out, and secure the side and bottom with pins.

4. Sew a ½" seam around the side and bottom edges, leaving the right side (which will become the top) open.

5. Knot the loose string ends together to secure.

YOU WILL NEED

- A cotton dish towel
- A piece of string (3" longer than length of towel)
- Straight pins
- Sewing machine
- Thread

How to Use

Before adding fresh greens, moisten the bag with cold water and wring out any excess moisture so the bag is damp, not dripping wet. Add the herbs, pull the drawstring to close and tuck the bag into your refrigerator's crisper section. Greens will stay crisp this way as long as you keep the bag lightly moistened.

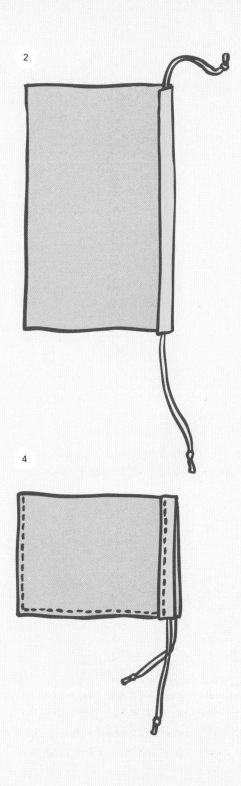

2

4

Herbs and Edible Flowers

Most people tend to toss a plastic bag of herbs into the fridge crisper, only to be faced with a pile of mush a few days later. Fresh, leafy herbs are a lot like greens, faring better when kept in a moist dish towel storage bag. For easy access, stand a handful in a cup of cold water placed in the fridge door and cut the leaves as you need them. Some herbs and flowers will last for weeks this way as long as you remember to change the water every few days. Basil is the exception, as its leaves will turn black in the fridge. However, it will stay fresh for nearly a week if set out on the counter in a vase or glass of water like a bouquet of flowers.

Long-Term Storage

Drying Vegetables and Fruit

An electric dehydrator is generally the way to go when drying most vegetables and fruit unless you live in an arid climate. The rest of us are stuck with dampness where mold and fungus growth are prone to start on air-drying produce before they get a chance to fully dehydrate.

Beans, onions, garlic, blueberries, and peppers are among the few items that can be air-dried just about anywhere very easily. Most of us don't have the climate for sun-dried tomatoes but can still pull off the real deal almost as easily in the oven (see "Oven-Dried Tomatoes," page 182). Tomatoes are by far my favorite food to dry. I promise, you will not regret making the effort.

Hang onions and garlic to dry (aka cure) by either tying or braiding the tops together in small bunches while the green parts are still flexible. Hang them for a month in a shady, dry spot such as a garage. Once cured, you can hang them in the kitchen for easy access or cut the tops off and store them somewhere cool for the long haul.

Any bean that has grown to maturity can be dried and saved for later, but some varieties are particularly prized for the way they retain their flavor and "meatiness" when dried. Shelled beans can be dried flat on top of a screen, or spare yourself the effort and just leave the pods to dry out on the vine, shelling them at your convenience later on. To shell a dried-bean windfall, toss the entire plant, pods still intact, into a burlap bag or pillowcase and then beat it with a broomstick or stomp on it with your feet. Try to use some restraint, because you want dried whole beans, not bean powder. To separate and sort the husks from the beans (aka *winnowing*), lay a sheet on the ground and set a basket on top. Holding a handful of beans high above the basket, slowly pour the beans into the basket, allowing the wind to blow away some of the dried pods. This works best (naturally) on a windy day. Store beans in clean Mason jars.

Wash, Don't Wash

It's okay to wash the dirt off peppers, tomatoes, and other thick-skinned vegetables before drying as long as you make sure to pat them down with a towel immediately afterward. Don't try to wash onions, garlic, shallots, or other vegetables with a papery, peel-away skin. The dirt will either fall off during the drying process or come off with the peel anyway. Similarly, soft fruit tends to turn mushy once wet. Because you're growing organically, there are no pesticides that need to be washed off anyway.

◀ String up a big hot pepper harvest into a decorative *ristra* (see page 184) and pluck as needed.

DRYING HERBS AND EDIBLE FLOWERS

- Harvest on a dry day when there is very little moisture on the leaves that could cause drying bundles of herbs to go moldy.

- Hang the bundles in a dry place with good air circulation and very little light.

- If the air is dusty and polluted, poke holes in a brown paper bag and tie it over a bundle of herbs before hanging.

- Store fully dried herbs and flowers in glass jars set in a dark cupboard.

- Label the jars, including the harvest date to keep track of freshness, and throw out old herbs after about a year or so.

- Crumble herbs lightly for storage purposes, but wait to fully grind or crush them until just before use so that they will hold their flavor longer.

HOLEY HOSIERY ONION HOLDER

Here's a ridiculously easy way to store a whole heap of onions and offer a second life to a holey pair of panty hose. To begin, cut the legs off a clean pair of old hosiery. The color doesn't matter, but thinner panty hose breathe better than thick, opaque tights. Pop an onion into one of the cut legs and tie a knot above it. Keep adding onions, tying a knot above each one until the leg is full.

Hang the onions to dry in a dry, dark, and cool place such as a closet, a corner of the garage, or a shed, because rows of dangling, bulbous panty hose may not be the look you're going for in the kitchen this fall.

When you're ready to use an onion, simply cut the bottom one off just below the first knot. A good keeping onion such as 'Ailsa Craig' or 'Yellow of Parma' will last stored this way for months.

Oven-Dried Tomatoes

If you've never tried drying your own tomatoes, you're missing out. The drying process condenses all the tomato sweetness into a savory and chewy piece of heaven. Those store-bought leathery things are good, but your own will be a million times better.

All that olive oil makes canning for long-term storage unsafe, but they're so good they never seem to sit around long enough anyway. I like to eat them piled on toast with a fresh basil leaf and slivers of good Parmesan cheese. You'll find your own way to enjoy them soon enough.

1. Preheat the oven to the lowest heat setting (150–200°F). The goal here is to dry the tomatoes slowly but surely.

2. Line a baking sheet with parchment paper. Arrange the tomatoes on top, cut side up. Sprinkle lightly with salt.

3. Bake the tomatoes until the edges have shriveled and the insides are still slightly moist but not juicy. Timing depends on the type and size of tomato; the drying will take anywhere between 2 and 8 hours.

4. Set the pan aside until completely cool and then transfer the tomatoes to a clean and sterilized jar. Add a few sprigs of dry herbs and a clove of garlic, if using, to the jar. Pour in olive oil, thoroughly covering the tomatoes to preserve them.

5. Store in the fridge for 4–6 weeks. Use up the remaining olive oil in dishes that can benefit from the savory tomato flavor.

- 10 plum tomatoes, halved
- Sea salt
- Dried thyme, oregano, or marjoram
- Garlic cloves, optional
- Approximately 2 cups olive oil

Dry grape and cherry tomatoes whole. Chop plum tomatoes in half. Cut large tomatoes into ½"-thick slices.

Makes 1 pint jar

Make a Ristra

Hot peppers are nothing if not prolific, often producing enough on each plant to upset the digestive systems of a small army. I am still in awe of a single plant that grew 200 peppers. Here's where stringing a *ristra* (pronounced REE-struh), a traditional southwestern dried pepper arrangement, comes in handy. Heavily shellacked versions are commonly seen hanging in Tex-Mex restaurants, but don't let associations with tacky décor put you off the real thing. A real *ristra* is a convenient way to store bundles of peppers for up to a year or more.

Do yourself a favor and wear protective gloves while handling hot peppers. Really hot peppers can actually burn your skin, and a bit of juice accidentally rubbed into an eye does not feel good.

CHOOSING HOT PEPPERS

Select only the best, blemish-free peppers with nice long stems still intact. Peppers with bad spots and bruises risk going moldy and contaminating the whole lot during the drying process. For quick and easy results, use small peppers with thin skins over large and meaty fruit.

YOU WILL NEED
- Approximately 50 hot peppers, stems attached
- Lightweight cotton string
- 1' lightweight wire (11–16 gauge)
- Pliers
- Latex gloves

1. Set your peppers aside to lose some moisture and loosen up for a day or two in a well-ventilated area. The stems of freshly picked peppers tend to be brittle and prone to breaking once you get started twisting and shaping the ristra.

2. To begin, tie a cluster of three peppers together by their stems. Hold the peppers by their stems and wrap the lightweight cotton string clockwise around the stems twice.

3. Next, holding the cluster so that one pepper is in front and two are behind, loop the string clockwise around the front pepper, bringing the string up between the cluster of peppers. Pull the string up tightly, cutting into the front pepper stem slightly to secure the string.

4. Loop the string around your hand and then give it a twist. Flip the loop over top of all three stems and pull tightly.

5. Repeating steps 3–5, tie another cluster of three peppers about 2–3 inches above the last one. Continue adding clusters until the string reaches 2'–5' in length. Make a shorter length when using large, heavy peppers and longer lengths for smaller peppers. Continue stringing peppers until they've all been used. If you want to make a mixed-pepper *ristra*, keep like with like, tying a single pepper variety onto its own string.

6. Make a small loop on both ends of the wire using a pair of pliers. Hang the wire from a secure spot that can withstand some weight. A hook or nail, doorknob, door frame, or strong clothesline will work.

7. Select a string of peppers to begin assembling the *ristra*. To make a mixed-pepper *ristra*, I prefer larger peppers at the bottom, working my way up the wire to smaller peppers at the top, but this is your project so anything goes.

(continued on next page)

(continued from previous page)

8. Set the first cluster of peppers just above and beside the loop at the bottom of the wire and braid the pepper stems and cotton string around the wire. I know this probably reads like craziness but I promise you that it will all make sense once you are actually doing it. The action is much like braiding hair, with the wire acting as one chunk of hair, and the pepper stems as the others. Twist the peppers and string around the wire until the cluster is securely in place.

9. Push each cluster of peppers down the length of the wire as it is braided so that the clusters sit nice and tight against each other. Move the peppers around if you like so that they stick out in different directions. Continue braiding in clusters, adding each string of peppers until they are all used.

10. *Ristras* are traditionally finished with a big piece of flair, usually cornhusk, raffia, or ribbon set on top like a giant cake topper. Alternatively, you can leave it simply as is: artist's choice.

11. Hang the completed *ristra* outside in full sun to dry. An open porch or deck with an overhang and good air circulation will work. A dry indoor location will work too. What's critical is that the *ristra* is not touching anything but has lots of airflow all around it to prevent mold.

12. Check your *ristra* occasionally and pull or cut off any peppers that rot. The drying process can take several weeks, but nothing should stop you from pulling peppers off and using them in the meantime. Just check for mold before tossing that pepper into an enchilada.

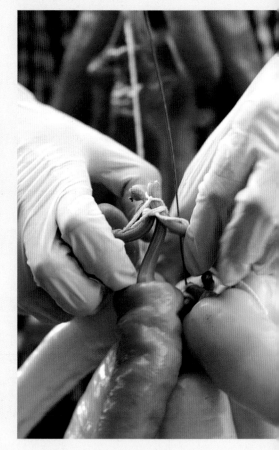

Putting on the Freeze

Freezing is one of the surest and safest ways to preserve that fresh flavor long-term. They don't call it "fresh frozen" for nothing. Your frozen goods are bound to be much fresher than the supermarket versions. Freezing is also pretty darn easy to do; some foods require little more than a few chops with a knife before hitting the deep freeze. Unfortunately it isn't exactly the most energy efficient way to go. For that reason it makes sense to reserve this kind of storage for the stuff that retains its straight-from-the-garden freshness after a stint in the old icebox, and save the rest for canning or drying methods that don't require a large electricity-sucking machine to keep.

▲
Chop off the tough skins of winter squash like 'Butternut' before blanching and freezing.

Freezing Vegetables and Fruit

Lots of veggies and fruit take well to a stretch in the freezer, including beans, beets, berries, broccoli, carrots, cauliflower, corn, melon, peaches, peas, peppers, rhubarb, spinach, tomatoes, and winter squash. Even apples and pears can be frozen as long as you peel and core them first, adding a splash of lemon juice to prevent discoloration. Stay away from veggies that are best eaten raw, such as cucumbers, lettuce, leafy greens, and radishes—the result is messy and kind of gross. Kale and collards will go soft but make a good addition to soups where mushiness won't matter.

TO FREEZE

Wash and chop tender, fresh-picked produce that isn't overripe. Berries, melons, and sweet peppers don't require blanching (a boiling-water bath), but most everything else does. Blanching stops enzymes in their tracks, preventing them from converting the sugars in recently harvested produce to bland and boring starch. It also helps food retain its nutritional value and integrity. See the next page for details.

Soft berries shoved into a bag or container inevitably freeze into a solid lump that melts into a mushy mass. Berries will stay whole and firm if you fast-freeze them whole on trays and package them up after they've been frozen.

HOW TO BLANCH FRUITS AND VEGETABLES

1. To blanch, plunge small quantities of chopped or whole produce into boiling water.

2. Put the lid on and wait for the water to come back to a boil and then begin to time the blanching process. The length of time depends on the size and type of produce (see above for approximate times).

3. Remove produce quickly with a slotted spoon and drop it into a bowl or sink filled with icy cold water to stop the cooking process quickly.

4. Once cool, drain and dry the goods before packaging in freezer bags or reusable freezer-safe containers. Stick to small, meal-sized portions and try to get as much air out of the package as possible, making sure the packages are sealed tightly.

VEGETABLE BLANCHING TIMES

Approximate blanching times are based on bite-sized pieces.

Beans: 1–3 minutes
Broccoli: 1–3 minutes
Carrots: 2 minutes
Cauliflower: 3 minutes
Corn (whole cob): 3–4 minutes
Peaches (whole): 1 minute
Peas: 1–3 minutes
Peppers: 2 minutes
Tomatoes (whole): 45 seconds
Winter squash: Thoroughly cook before freezing.

Freezing Herbs and Flowers

Fresh-freeze herbs such as basil, dill, cilantro, parsley, oregano, and tarragon by chopping the leaves and freezing them in ice cube trays topped up with water. Then pop them into freezer bags or freezable containers, where they'll be available in portion-controlled sizes. Herbs with textured leaves, including sage and rosemary, maintain their flavor, color, and texture when frozen whole. Simply sticking herbs such as basil, cilantro, or mint in a freezer bag preserves the flavor, but the herbs tend to turn out mushy and discolored, and dare I say, a little gross. This method works well for cooking—just chop off what you need and return to the rest to the freezer—but is not what you want in a garnish.

Despite that last paragraph of nay-saying, I do recommend processing batches of basil with lots of olive oil and a dash of salt. This cheese-and nut-free pestolike paste lasts for 8 months or longer in the freezer when tightly smushed into airless freezer bags.

Canning

The act of canning is genius. Food that tastes as good as fresh can be stored for months at a time without the use of electricity. There was a time—let's call it "the olden days"—when everyone had a pantry filled with lined-up jars of this, that, and the other all made at home using food they had grown. Fast-forward to "the future," where the norm is adults and kids who grew up as I did, unable to recognize food that doesn't come in a can or freezer tray. I was totally baffled, if not a little bit freaked, by the discovery of preserves in my great-grandmother's country house. It actually took me a good couple of minutes to figure out that the objects floating around in jars of colored liquid were peaches and tomatoes and not a horror film come to life.

The fact is that we're still a little bit suspicious of home-canned goods, and for good reason. A lot of the scary stuff you hear about botulism and other potentially fatal food-related illnesses is no joke and should be taken seriously. But with some safety precautions and care, even the smallest apartment dweller can build up a small stash of snack foods for the apocalypse and have fun doing it too!

TIPS FOR CAUTIOUS CANNING

- Follow up-to-date recipes and procedures published within the last decade or so. Vintage canning pamphlets are often off the mark when it comes to contemporary safety standards.

- Get your feet wet jarring high-acid preserves like pickles, and then move on to other safe and easy foods like tomatoes and applesauce once you've gained experience.

- Do not attempt to preserve low-acid vegetables (i.e., beans and carrots) in water unless you've got a pressure canner. Safely canning low-acid food requires a very high heat that can't be reached with a standard boiling-water-bath canner.

- Stick to small batches that are less pressure and panic inducing.

- Too nervous to try long-term canning? Make small batches of pickles, chutneys, and jellies for the fridge that will be eaten in a few weeks tops.

Gearing Up

Stay safe by using good-quality gear. Used and vintage equipment can be okay, but the jar lids should always be new to ensure the best and safest seal possible. Stay away from used mayo, pickle, or other commercial jars because they aren't made to withstand the wear and tear of home canning and are less likely to seal properly.

If you plan to can even one time and do not have someone to borrow equipment from, do yourself a favor and buy a home canning kit. Even a simple kit from the hardware store will make your life easier and the canning experience about a hundred times more enjoyable. First, buy a canning kettle that comes with a rack. Sure, a large kettle pot will do, but you will be cursing yourself when it comes time to juggle hot jars and boiling water with nothing but a cheap pair of tongs. A rack allows you to pull several jars out in one quick motion. Hooray!

Pick up an all-in-one canning kit that includes tongs, a jar lifter, a canning funnel, and a magnetic lid wand. I promise you, that kit will start earning its keep immediately.

From around the home you'll need clean towels, paper towels, a timer, and an air bubble remover. Wooden chopsticks or plastic takeout cutlery serve this function perfectly.

ABOUT PECTIN

Jelly recipes in this book call for low-methoxyl pectin instead of the ordinary stuff. Regular pectin requires exceptionally high sugar content (55 percent or more) to make jellies and jams that are firmly "set" or gelled. Low-methoxyl pectin opens up a world of opportunities, allowing you to use alternative sweeteners such as honey or agave syrup, or even none at all, yet still achieve a hard gel. I use a brand called Pomona's Universal Pectin, a product derived from citrus pectin that is available in most health food stores.

Let's Get It On

Canning is a bit like a well-choreographed dance. The timing of each movement is key to the success of the whole. It takes a bit of practice to get into step with the rhythm, so don't worry if you're a bit clumsy and awkward on your first time out. Trust me, once you get the hang of it you'll actually have fun. These are general directions. You should always follow the specific recipes for each since they differ.

STERILIZING

Wash lids and jars in hot, soapy water. Next, half-fill your canning pot with hot water and bring to a boil. Once it is boiling, submerge the jars and screw bands for 10–15 minutes to sterilize. Heat lids (the part with the rubber seal) in very hot water for 5 minutes, but do not boil. Turn off the heat and keep the jars warm in the hot water right up until the moment you're ready to fill them.

FILLING

Using clean tongs or a spoon, carefully arrange or scoop the produce (according to recipe directions) into each jar. Next, fill the jars with pickling solution, jelly, jam or other preserving liquid (if called for). Rather than filling the jars right up to the top, leave a bit of headspace to allow for expansion during the sterilizing process. It's important to follow recipe directions to the letter here because too little or too much headspace can wreak havoc on the sealing process.

CAPPING

Once jars are filled you'll need to remove any air bubbles. Run a plastic knife or other nonmetallic cutlery around the inside of the jar to release trapped air. Wipe off the rim of the jar with a damp paper towel or clean damp cloth. Remove a still-warm lid from the water bath using a magnetic lid wand (aren't you glad you got one?) and place it on top of the jar. Lightly hold the lid in place with one finger while twisting the screw band on top. Don't go overboard with the muscles; a bit of resistance is good enough.

Canning Labels: Regular ol' metal jar lids aren't good enough for your beautiful preserves! Gussy up tacky canning lids with labels like the ones I include on page 203. Make color photocopies, or scan and print the labels onto self-sticking paper and adhere to the top of your jars.

Suitable for Canning: The following recipes found in this book are safe for home canning: Tangy Red Pepper Ketchup (page 105), 'Dark Opal' Basil Jelly (page 147), Better-Than-Canned Heirloom Tomatoes (page 194), Herb and Flower Vinegars (page 196), and Everything but the Kitchen Sink Pickle (page 198).

Stay safe and stick to jars that are made specifically for home canning. Thrift store jars are great but always buy lids new.

HEAT PROCESSING

This next step, called *heat processing* or the *boiling-water bath* is an important one because it creates the vacuum seal and destroys any lingering microorganisms that may have been introduced into the jars during the packing process.

When all of your jars are packed, capped, and ready to rumble, gently place them upright on the rack in the canning pot, making sure that the jars are not bumping up against each other. Check that the jars are completely submerged with at least 2" of water above them. Cover the canner and bring the water to a boil. Start your timer only after the water has started to boil.

Note: Because water boils at lower temperatures in higher altitudes, you may need to boil your jars for a longer period if you live at a higher elevation. Add 1 additional minute to the processing time for every 1,000 feet above sea level.

COOLING OFF

When the timer goes off, turn off the heat and allow everything to settle before lifting the jars out of the water using the jar lifter. Set the jars on a wooden board to cool and wait for that famous popping sound that signals a successful seal.

Check back in 24 hours to be sure that a sealing vacuum has formed within each jar. Push down lightly on the center of each lid. If it is down and stays down when pushed, it is safe to store. Move jars that fail to seal into the fridge and eat the contents right away.

Storing Canned Goods

Keep your jars in a cool, dry, and dark place. Special cupboards or pantry shelves are wonderful, but not always available to those of us who are short on space. Instead, pack the jars back into the segmented boxes they came in and tuck them under the bed or couch, or in a deep closet. Just don't forget where you put them!

Eat everything up before a year has passed.

SIGNS OF SPOILAGE

Check your jars for these telling danger signs before serving them with lunch or, oh dear, giving them to friends. Throw out the offending jar immediately without hesitation and wash your hands before doing anything else!

Tiny Bubbles: Bubbles, even little ones, are cute and fun in champagne but a sign of foul play in canned goods. Dispose of anything that gives off a gas when you open the jar.

Color Shifts: First it was apricot, but now it's amber. Garlic and cauliflower are prone to a natural color shift when pickled (a reaction with the vinegar); however, a significant color change in preserves such as jellies may mean trouble.

Mold: Whether in the jar or out, this can only mean one thing—toss it. Check for mold on the lid or inside the contents. Mold on the outside can be an indication that the food inside has gone bad and leaked out.

Slimy: You definitely don't want to mess with pickles that have taken on a slimy texture. Yuck.

Oils in Canning: Even a little bit of oil can lower the pH of your recipe. To be safe, keep oil out of recipes intended for the home canner.

Better-Than-Canned Heirloom Tomatoes

- 5 pounds heirloom tomatoes
- Lemon juice

Save the very best tomatoes for preserving. Overripe, rotten, bruised, or mushy tomatoes may actually lower the pH or spoil. Red, black, and some orange tomatoes are your best bet because most other colored varieties tend to be much less acidic. Can individual varieties in their own jar and label each jar so you know what you're enjoying six months down the road.

Growing up, my brother and I were often forced to eat mushy, commercially canned tomatoes mashed into mac and cheese made from a box. Memories of that repulsive meal put me off the idea of home-canned tomatoes until I finally took a chance recently and made my own. This recipe provides an easy introduction to canning; even beginners will be able to handle this project.

Canning your tomatoes simply with no added ingredients means you'll always have tomatoes on hand whenever a recipe requires them.

1. Sterilize several pint canning jars, lids, and screw bands according to the directions on page 191.

2. Bring 1 quart of soft tap water or bottled distilled water to a boil. This will be used to top off the jars of tomatoes.

3. Remove the tomato skins by blanching the tomatoes for 45 seconds according to the directions on page 188.

4. Once the tomatoes are cool, slide their skins off and cut out the core with a sharp knife. Dice up large tomatoes into 2" pieces and set aside in a large bowl. Keep small tomatoes whole.

5. Pack the tomatoes into the sterilized jars, filling to within ½" of the top. Use a canning funnel if the jar is narrow at the top.

6. Add 1 tablespoon lemon juice to each jar. Pour in enough boiling water to fill the gaps between tomatoes, making sure to maintain ½" headspace.

7. Cap the jars and heat-process in a boiling-water bath for 45 minutes according to the directions on page 192.

Makes 7–9 pint jars

Acid Bath: Preserving with Vinegar

The high acid content of vinegar makes it a supreme way to keep nasty microorganisms at bay. On the bright side, just about everything, including herbs, veggies, soft berries, and watermelon rind, tastes really good after a long soak in vinegar. Unfortunately, it's not the most nutritious way to store food. There's a reason why no one has ever launched a total pickle diet: all that acid, often accompanied by a ton of salt, tends to suck healthy vitamins and minerals right out of quality food. Luckily, most of us reserve pickles and vinegars to condiment-sized portions, with the occasional assault on a jar of dill pickled cukes. Try your hand at the following recipes and once you're a pro, step out with confidence and creativity into a whole wild world of pickling.

The colorful combination of red onions and purple cauliflower turned this homemade pickle nuclear pink.

Make copycat capers using nasturtium buds. Pluck the buds when they are just beginning to form and are tightly closed. Submerge in a covered bowl of white wine vinegar for a week and then can in a sealed jar following the safe-canning procedures outlined on pages 189–92.

Herb and Flower Vinegars

- 2½ cups vinegar
- A handful or two of fresh or dried herbs, enough to fill the jar

Take your vinegar a step beyond by adding little hot peppers, garlic cloves, whole peppercorns, spices, or even soft berries.

Overdecorated gifts swathed in raffia and fake flowers gave herbal vinegars a bad rap in the 1990s, but if anything is worth a comeback, this is it. A splash of acidic flavored vinegar makes a drab meal come alive. Toss a little into sauces or use it in veggie and meat marinades. Use your own special brew to create unique-tasting pickles, homemade mustard, and mayonnaise. Keep a bottle or two on hand to use wherever regular vinegar is called for.

1. Simmer the vinegar over medium-low heat so that it is warm but nowhere near boiling. Your aim is to draw the flavor from the herbs, not cook them. Use a stainless steel, enamel, or glass pot because vinegar can react with other metals.

2. Cut up or crumble fresh or dried herbs into 2"–3" pieces and stuff them into a clean, pint-sized canning jar. Lightly crush seeds and hard stems to get more from your herbs.

3. Cover the herbs completely with warm vinegar. Before capping the jar tightly, use a cork or put a piece of protective plastic or waxed paper between the jar and the metal lid—vinegar can corrode the metal!

4. Set the jar in a dark spot for a week or two until the vinegar smells fragrant and tastes delicious. Herbs with delicate flower parts (nasturtiums) require a week or less; herbs with woody stems (rosemary) are best after a long soak. If the vinegar still seems weak, strain the old herbs through a coffee filter, replace with a fresh batch, and set aside the vinegar to soak a little longer.

5. When the vinegar smells and tastes ready, strain out the herb bits and pour the vinegar into a new, clean jar. Sterilize the jar if you plan to keep the vinegar for a month or more. See page 191 for directions on how to sterilize jars.

Makes 1 pint

CHOOSING INGREDIENTS

Good ingredients create good results. Choose only the best fresh or dried herbs. Use rice wine vinegar or white wine vinegar for their mellow, almost fruity tang. Cider vinegar works well with strong herbs, but skip the regular distilled white vinegar, whose flavor is too pedestrian for your hard-won herbs.

The sky's the limit when choosing and combining flavors to infuse. Try the deep flavor of 'African Blue' basil, sage, nasturtium, or bee balm. Unusual herbs like salad burnet, chervil, and mint are tasty too. Purple basils and shiso make cheery, colorful vinegars, while nasturtiums turn out a nuclear orange liquid. Experiment with the seeds, flowers, stems, and leaves.

HERBAL BLENDS TO TRY

Tangy Bite: Dill, nasturtium, lemon balm
Lemony: Lemon basil, lemongrass, lemon thyme
Italian Herb: Basil, oregano, thyme
Scarborough Fair: Parsley, sage, rosemary, thyme
Purple Basils: 'Purple Ruffles', 'Thai', 'Cinnamon' basil
Cool Blue Cucumber: Borage flowers, salad burnet
Fruity Fennel: Fennel seeds, shiso

Everything but the Kitchen Sink Pickle

There was a time about a decade ago when I was known—albeit mostly in my own head—as the Pickle Queen, a self-appointed title I did not take lightly. My obsession with making the perfect pickle ended at the start of 2000 when I achieved my ultimate goal, the Millennium Pickle, a recipe I foolishly forgot to write down. Just recently the desire to soak vegetables in vinegar was suddenly reignited for no reason at all.

This recipe is perfect for us small-space gardeners because we are less likely to have an overabundance of any one pickling ingredient but often have a whole lot of this and that. Replace any of the vegetables used in this recipe with whatever you've got on hand. Just about any combination will work. These pickles look really pretty in a jar, turning a bright neon pink when you use red onions and purple cauliflower. Add hot peppers if you like your pickles spicy.

OPTIONAL INGREDIENTS

Sliced beets, sliced Jerusalem artichokes, cucumbers, garlic, asparagus.

1. Sterilize six pint canning jars, lids, and screw bands according to the directions on page 191.

2. Fill a large pot with water and set it to boil on high. Set a large bowl of ice-cold water in the sink. This setup will be used to blanch the cauliflower and carrot.

3. Chop the cauliflower into 1" florets and slice the carrot into 1/8"-thick coins. Blanch them separately in small batches for about 2–3 minutes, followed by a quick plunge in the ice-cold water. Drain and set aside.

4. Prepare the remaining vegetables for pickling. Cut the ends off the wax beans and dice into 1" bits. Slice the black radish thin just like the carrots. Slice the onion into thin slivers and chop the sweet peppers into 1" chunks. The hot peppers, if using, can be kept whole or cut into smaller pieces.

5. Add ¼ teaspoon black mustard seeds, ¼ teaspoon dill seeds, 4 black peppercorns, and 1 sprig fresh dill to each jar.

6. Pack the jars with a little bit of each vegetable, filling to within an inch of the top.

7. Bring the vinegar, the kosher salt, and 4½ cups distilled water to a boil, stirring until the salt is dissolved.

8. Pour the hot vinegar mixture into each jar, leaving ½" of headspace.

9. Cap and seal the jars according to the directions on pages 191–192 and heat-process the jars in a boiling-water bath for 15 minutes.

Makes 6 pints

- 1 small cauliflower
- 1 red carrot
- ½ pound yellow wax beans
- 1 black radish
- 1 onion
- ½ pound sweet peppers
- 4 hot peppers, optional
- 1½ teaspoons black mustard seeds
- 1½ teaspoons dill seeds
- 24 black peppercorns
- 6 dill sprigs
- 3 cups vinegar
- 6 tablespoons pickling salt

If you'd rather not bother with sterilizing jars, reduce the batch size and keep the pickles in the fridge. They will last about a month.

Resources

Canning

- Ball (homecanning.com)
- Lehman's (lehmans.com)
- Pomona's Universal Pectin (pomonapectin.com)
- Weck (weckcanning.com)
- *Well Preserved*, Mary Anne Dragan (1998, Whitecap)

Citrus Trees

- Dwarf citrus trees: Four Winds Growers (fourwindsgrowers.com)

Community Gardening

- American Community Gardening Association (communitygarden.org)
- *Community Gardening*, Ellen Kirby and Elizabeth Peters (2008, Brooklyn Botanic Garden)
- Green Thumb (greenthumbnyc.org)
- *How Does Our Garden Grow? A Guide to Community Garden Success*, Laura Berman (1997, Food Share; foodshare.net)

Composting and Soil

- *Compost: The Natural Way to Make Food for Your Garden*, Ken Thompson (2007, DK)
- *Rodale Organic Gardening Basics: Soil* (2000, Rodale)
- *Worms Eat My Garbage*, Mary Appelhof (1982, Flower)
- *You Grow Girl: The Groundbreaking Guide to Gardening*, Gayla Trail (2005, Fireside). See pages 50 and 96 for instructions on composting and building a worm bin.

Food Security

- *Animal, Vegetable, Miracle: A Year of Food Life*, Barbara Kingsolver (2008, HarperPerennial)
- *Gardening When It Counts: Growing Food in Hard Times*, Steve Solomon (2006, New Society)
- *The 100-Mile Diet: A Year of Local Eating*, Alisa Smith and J. B. MacKinnon (2007, Random House Canada)
- *In Defense of Food: An Eater's Manifesto*, Michael Pollan (2008, Penguin)

Garden Pests and Diseases

- *The Organic Gardener's Handbook of Natural Insect and Disease Control*, edited by Barbara W. Ellis and Fern Marshall Bradley (1996, Rodale)

Micro Greens Sources

- Botanical Interests (botanicalinterests.com)—Micro Greens: Mild Mix, Micro Greens: Spicy Mix
- Urban Harvest (uharvest.ca)—Spicy Salad Mix, Mild Salad Mix

Miscellaneous Organic Gardening Supplies

- Gardener's Supply Company (gardeners.com)
- Gardens Alive (gardensalive.com)
- Natural Gardener (naturalgardeneraustin.com)
- I've stopped using rooting hormones; they're really not necessary. But if you'd rather use one, try a natural product like Root-A-Maker Natural Rooting Powder from Richters (richters.com)

Seed Purchase

UNITED STATES

- Baker Creek Heirloom Seeds (rareseeds.com)
- Bountiful Gardens (bountifulgardens.org)
- The Cook's Garden (cooksgarden.com)
- Renee's Garden (reneesgarden.com)
- Seeds of Change (seedsofchange.com)
- Territorial Seed Company (territorialseed.com)
- Tomato Growers Supply Company (tomatogrowers.com)

CANADA

- Greta's Organic Gardens (seeds-organic.com)
- Salt Spring Seeds (saltspringseeds.com)
- Terra Edibles (terraedibles.ca)
- Urban Harvest (uharvest.ca)
- West Coast Seeds (westcoastseeds.com)

INTERNATIONAL

- Kokopelli Seed Foundation (kokopelli-seed-foundation.com)

Seed Saving

- *How to Save Your Own Seeds: A Handbook for Home Seed Production*, edited by Heather Apple (2005, Seeds of Diversity Canada)
- *Seed to Seed: Seed Saving and Growing Techniques for Vegetable Gardeners*, Suzanne Ashworth (2002, Seed Savers Exchange)

Seed Trading

UNITED STATES

- Saving Our Seeds (savingourseeds.org)
- Seed Savers Exchange (seedsavers.org)

CANADA

- Seeds of Diversity Canada (seeds.ca)
- Seedy Saturday (seeds.ca/ev/events.php)

Trash Can Spuds: Certified Seed Potato Suppliers

- Seeds of Change (seedsofchange.com)
- Vesey's (veseys.com)
- Wilton's Organic Potatoes: Seed Savers (seedsavers.org)

Seed Starting and Planting Chart

- Write the "Date of Last Frost" for your region in the space provided (see almanac.com).
- Using a calendar, calculate the "Planting Date" by adding or subtracting the "Safe Set Out" (number of weeks listed) from the "Date of Last Frost."
- Calculate the "Sow Date" by subtracting the "Growth Period" from the "Planting Date."

CROP	SOW DATE	GROWTH PERIOD	SAFE SET OUT	PLANTING DATE
VEGGIES				
• Beans			2 weeks after	
• Beets			2 weeks before	
Broccoli		6 weeks	3 weeks before	
Cabbage		6 weeks	3 weeks before	
• Carrot			1–2 weeks before	
Cauliflower		4–6 weeks	At last frost	
Cucumber		2–4 weeks	1–2 weeks after	
Eggplant		6–9 weeks	3 weeks after	
• Lettuce & Greens			Workable soil	
• Kale			4 weeks before	
Leeks		10–12 weeks	1 week after	
• Onion			2–3 weeks before	
• Peas			4–6 weeks before	
Pepper		8–10 weeks	2 weeks after	
• Potato			2 weeks before	
Pumpkin		3–4 weeks	2–3 weeks before	
• Radish			3–4 weeks before	
• Spinach			3–6 weeks before	
Squash		2–4 weeks	2 weeks after	
• Swiss Chard			2 weeks before	
Tomato		6–8 weeks	1 week after	
EDIBLE FLOWERS & HERBS				
Basil		5–7 weeks	2 weeks after	
• Calendula			0–1 week after	
• Cilantro			Workable soil	
• Dill			Workable soil	
• Nasturtium			0–2 weeks after	
Parsley		8–10 weeks	2 weeks before	
• Sunflower			0–1 week after	
• **DATE OF LAST FROST:**				

• Indicates direct-sown seeds

Canning Labels

- Photocopy or scan this page at 100%.
- Alternatively, download a printable pdf (see yougrowgirl.com).
- Print onto self-stick paper.

Glossary

- **Annuals** are flowering plants that complete their life cycle within one year from germination to death. They germinate, develop leaves and roots, flower, produce seeds, and die within one year.
- **Biennials** are flowering plants that complete their life cycle within two years. They germinate and grow leaves and roots within the first year, then produce flowers and seeds before dying in the second year.
- **Bolting** occurs when crops such as lettuce, radish, and spinach produce flowers and seeds, prematurely triggered by bright sun and heat.
- **Cross-pollination** is the transfer of pollen between two different plants.
- **Hardiness** refers to a plant's ability to withstand temperature extremes. A plant described as "hardy" can survive very cold winter weather.
- **Heirlooms** are open-pollinated plant varieties that have remained unchanged in an area for at least 50–100 years.
- **Hybrid plants** are varieties that have been crossbred in a controlled environment between two closely related species to create specific results. Hybrids are typically bred to be hardy in extreme weather or less susceptible to diseases and insect pests. Hybrids are often indicated by "F1" on seed packets.
- **Microclimates** are pockets of localized conditions where the climate differs from the larger surrounding area. Ponds, sidewalks, walls, metal fire escapes, tall buildings, trees, plants, and roads are just some factors that can alter conditions within a garden space.
- **Open-pollinated plants** are varieties that have developed as a result of natural pollination. They are indicated by "OP" on seed packets.
- **Perennials** are flowering plants that live for more than two years and do not die after flowering.
- **Pot up** means to plant a transplant into a container or pot.
- **Seed leaves** are the first set of leaves to appear when a seed germinates. Although they may look like leaves, they are actually an embryonic food supply that is a part of the seed, called cotyledon leaves.
- **Self-pollinators** are plants that can successfully pollinate themselves and produce fruit (or seeds) with only one plant.
- **Self-sowing plants** produce seeds and germinate without human assistance.
- **Species** are a group of plants with common characteristics that can be crossbred with one another.
- **Tender** describes a plant that cannot withstand frost conditions.
- **True leaves** are the first set of actual leaves that appear after the seed leaves.
- **Varieties** are subcategories of a species that have different characteristics such as leaf color, fruit color, or shape.
- **Volunteers** are plants that appear where they have not been planted intentionally, usually the result of self-sowing.
- **Water in** describes the act of watering a newly planted seedling or plant. When watering in, be sure to really soak the soil around the roots of the plant to ensure that it gets well established in its new home.

Acknowledgments

Big love to everyone who has stopped by YouGrowGirl.com through the years and shared their gardening life. Extra shout outs to the old-growth peeps (and especially Shay) who have been there since the very beginning!

Endless sloppy thank-yous to Davin Risk, my creative partner (and more), who worked so hard on illustrations, design, photographs, gardening. This is his book as much as it is mine.

A promise of future pickles and sauce to Jen for listening, advising, and being such a supportive friend.

Thanks to my professional support system, Laura Nolan and Sarah Sockit Moseley, for believing in me and turning that belief into something tangible. And to Clarkson Potter, specifically Aliza Fogelson for going the extra mile.

To gardening comrades new and old with whom I can boldly and brazenly share a love of this crazy world of plants (and often more): Sakurako Handa, Gwynne Basen, Margaret Roach, Renee Garner, Amy Urqhuart, Lorraine Johnson, Beate Schwirtlich, Keri Smith, Colette Murphy, Laura Berman, Julie Jackson, Scott Meyer, Kelly Gilliam, Julianna, Myla Kent, Ravenna Barker, Sapphire Singh, and Sarah Hood. And many more still who have so warmly and enthusiastically (and bravely) invited me into their gardens with my cameras.

To the best market in the world, the Dufferin Grove, and the farmers whose good food fills in the gaps my small gardens can't meet. And to coffee: your delicious flavor kept me going through many long nights. Espresso-based, organically grown, free trade goodness only. None of that drip rubbish.

Credits

Photography: Gayla Trail and Davin Risk
Illustration: Davin Risk

Index

Note: page numbers in **bold** indicate the main discussion of a plant; page numbers in *italics* refer to photographs.